HAPPINESS

How to Find It

Most people fail to find happiness. But that need not be true in your case. The experience of persons around the globe proves that contentment and a rewarding life are within your reach. We publish this book to make available the valuable information you need to find happiness.

—The Publishers

Publishers
WATCHTOWER BIBLE AND TRACT SOCIETY
OF NEW YORK, INC.
INTERNATIONAL BIBLE STUDENTS ASSOCIATION
BROOKLYN, NEW YORK, U.S.A.

This Book Is Published in 31 Languages
Total Books Printed of All Editions:
16,360,000 Copies

Happiness—How to Find It
English (*hp*-E)
Made in the United States of America

CONTENTS

NOTE: Bible quotations in this book are from the modern-language *New World Translation of the Holy Scriptures,* revised edition of 1971.

In connection with dates, the abbreviation B.C.E. means "Before the Common Era," and C.E. means "Of the Common Era."

1

Is a Happy Life Really Possible?

"IT'S good to be alive!" That is the way a person feels when he is happy. But if we are realistic, we know that life is not always that way. There are problems. These may be so many and so weighty that real happiness seems just a dream. Need it be that way?

² You know that a happy life is made up of various elements. To enjoy life we need enough to eat, and suitable clothing. We need a home where we can find protection and rest. Yet these are just the basics. Pleasant companionship and good health are also important.

³ But even those who have a measure of these things may still long for true happiness. The type of work a person does, or the conditions under which he must work, may rob him of contentment. Also, in many families there is conflict between husband and wife or between parents and children. Nor can we ignore that over all of us hangs the possibility of sickness or sudden death. Do you believe that it is possible to cope with these and other problems in such a way that we can find true satisfaction? There is reason to believe so. Yet for anyone to enjoy a happy life, he first needs something that not all have—a *reason* to live.

POINT FOR DISCUSSION: What is needed to be happy in life? (1-10)

[4] Your life must have meaning if you are to be truly happy. In his book *The Transparent Self,* Professor S. M. Jourard writes:

"A person lives as long as he experiences his life as having meaning and value and as long as he has something to live *for* . . . As soon as meaning, value and hope vanish from a person's experience, he begins to stop living; he begins to die."

This is now being recognized even in industry. A Canadian report on job absenteeism commented:

"People are looking for meaning in their lives and are no longer satisfied to be dispensable faceless cogs in the machinery of society."—*Atlas World Press Review.*

[5] This helps to explain why many of the wealthy are not really satisfied. Oh, yes, they eat, sleep, have a family and share some of life's pleasures and comforts. But they may sense that the same could be said of many animals. There must be more to life.

[6] Nor is just long life the answer. Many elderly persons know from experience that a long life without a feeling of accomplishment or of being needed is wearisome. Have you seen that?

[7] The lack of an ennobling reason to live is not confined to persons up in years. A survey conducted by Japan's Daito Bunka University revealed that, of 1,500 high school students, 50 percent of the girls and 34 percent of the boys had already considered suicide. Why? First among the reasons given was "the meaninglessness of life." And is it much different in Europe, in the Americas and in Africa? The worldwide rise in suicide shows that more and more persons are unhappy and have given up on life.

know why evil exists, if it will end, and, if so, how. And he would know what we can do to make our lives happier and more meaningful. So, then, 'Does God exist?'

A PERPLEXED MAN

A man in Japan named Yamamoto relates:

"While preparing for college entrance examinations a few years ago, I spent much of my time contemplating the meaning and purpose of life. The more I studied books on philosophy, the more disappointed I was. After passing my examination I joined a political party. But seeing all the badness around me, I again faced the question, 'What is the purpose of life?'"

He did not find satisfying answers in the philosophies of men, who clearly have not solved mankind's problems. Nor did his study of history or his experience with politics indicate that any human government holds the answer. Men have tried all sorts of governments, yet the question regarding the meaning of life persisted. The Japanese man adds:

"I began to live a pleasure-seeking life, doing so half out of despair. But I soon sensed the folly of that. I finally came to the conclusion that the answer to my long-perplexing question regarding the reason or purpose for life depended upon whether God exists or not."

2

Does It Make Sense to Believe in God?

ONE of the most important questions you will ever face is, 'Does God exist?' The conclusion you reach can affect your view of your family, work, money, morality and even life itself.

² If asked, 'Does God exist?' many persons would reply by repeating what they have read or heard from others. However, you *personally* should give thought to the question. In his book *Man, God and Magic,* Dr. Ivar Lissner observes that a "fundamental difference between man and beast" is that "man is not content merely to sleep, eat and warm himself." Man has a "strange and inherent urge" that can be called "spirituality." Dr. Lissner adds that 'all the civilizations of mankind have been rooted in a quest for God.' So your coming to grips with the question, 'Does God exist?' is an evidence that you have not neglected an important attribute—your spirituality.

³ How could you go about determining whether there is a 'maker and ruler of the universe, a Supreme Being,' as one dictionary defines "God"? Well, reason indicates that if there is a 'maker of the universe,' there should be indications of its beginning, also evidence of design and order.

POINT FOR DISCUSSION: Why should we consider, 'Does God exist?' (1-3)

In your examining whether there are such, we invite you to consider what biologists have found about life and what has been learned about our universe by physicists and astronomers using telescopes and space probes.

YOUR LIFE—IS CHANCE RESPONSIBLE?

4 Why not begin with yourself? Where did your life come from? True, it was passed on by your parents. But how did life on earth originate?

5 In an effort to produce life in a laboratory and thus explain how it began, chemists have sent sparks through mixtures of special gases. One result has been some amino acids (molecules of the sort that are the 'building blocks' of living things). Those amino acids, though, were not living. Furthermore, they were not the result of mere accident; they were produced by trained scientists under controlled conditions in modern laboratories.

6 There are more than 200 natural amino acids, yet only a special 20 in the proteins of living things. Even *if* some amino acids could result from lightning, who selected just the right 20 found in living matter? And how were they guided into the exact sequence necessary in protein? Research analyst Dr. J. F. Coppedge calculated that 'the probability of just *one* protein molecule resulting from a chance arrangement of amino acids is 1 in 10^{287}.' (That is a figure with 287 zeros after it.) Additionally, he points out that, not one, but 'a minimum of 239 protein molecules are required for the smallest theoretical form of life.' Do you think that such evidence points to life as resulting from blind chance, or is it from intelligent design?

To what does life on earth point? (4-9)

[7] Consider also another type of laboratory experiment that has been publicized in newspapers as "creating life." With complex equipment scientists have taken a virus produced by a living organism and separated the components. Later they have taken these components and reunited them into a virus. However, biologist René Dubos explains in the *Encyclopædia Britannica* that it is really a mistake to call this feat "creating life." Neither these scientists nor others have been able to make new life from inanimate material. Rather than suggesting that life comes from chance, this experiment showed that "all the biological machinery" needed for life "had to be provided by preexisting life."

[8] Even if scientists could produce living protein from inanimate matter, it would simply confirm that preexisting intelligent life was needed as a directing force. Obviously, humans were not here to begin life on earth. Yet life was created, including human life. Who is responsible? Bible writers long ago came to a conclusion that merits serious consideration. One said: "The breath of the Almighty gave me life." Another added: "[God] is himself the universal giver of life."*

[9] A closer look at your body will help you to reason further on this.

YOUR CELLS—YOUR BRAIN—YOU
[10] Life throbs in your body, made up of about 100,000,000,000,000 tiny cells. The cell is the basic component of every living thing on earth. The

---

* Job 33:4; Acts 17:25, *New English Bible.*

What can we learn about our cells that helps when considering the existence of God? (10-14)

YOUR CELLS

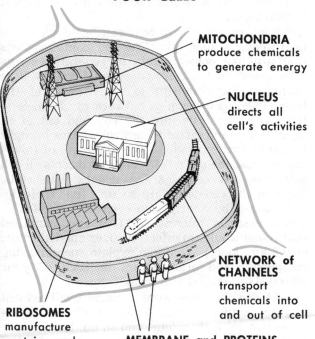

MITOCHONDRIA
produce chemicals
to generate energy

NUCLEUS
directs all
cell's activities

NETWORK of CHANNELS
transport
chemicals into
and out of cell

RIBOSOMES
manufacture
proteins and
hormones for
shipment to other
parts of body

MEMBRANE and PROTEINS
control what is brought
in and battle invaders

"Today at least 80% of the scientists who deal with biology would probably admit that biology and life are regulated by some higher power.

"The superb order and regulation in various manifestations of life and in the basic processes at the cellular and molecular levels have strong influence on the belief that a higher power exists."
—"Journal of the American Medical Association."

more carefully it is studied, the more complex it is seen to be.

[11] Each of your body cells can be likened to a microscopic walled city. The cell contains parts that are like power plants to generate energy. "Factories" in the cell make proteins as well as hormones for shipment to other parts of the body. There is a complex network of channels to transport chemicals into the cell and out of it. "Sentries" stand guard to control what is brought in and to battle invaders. The key to all of this is the nucleus, the cell's "city hall." It directs all cell activities and contains the genetic blueprints. Some of the cell parts are so tiny that their details cannot be clearly seen even with a 200,000-power electron microscope. (An ant magnified that much would, in effect, be over one-half mile, or 0.8 km, long.) What can explain such amazing complexity and organization in each of your 100,000,000,000,000 tiny cells?

[12] At one time you were a single fertilized cell in your mother's womb. That cell divided to become two cells, then four, and so on. Later, some of those cells became muscle tissue. Others formed your eyes, bones and heart. How was it that the cells formed each of your body parts at the right time and location? Why, for example, did cells develop into ears where they belonged, and not on your knee or your arm?

[13] Look even more closely. In every cell you have tens of thousands of genes and the vital DNA, which tells the cell how to function and reproduce. It is said that the DNA in each cell contains enough information to fill an encyclopedia of 1,000 volumes. It determined the color of your hair, how fast you grew, the width of your smile

HER BRAIN
   enables her to—

Balance the bicycle

Hear approaching cars

Smell the flowers

Feel the breeze

Watch the dog

Remember the way home

and countless other details about you. All of that was 'written down' in the DNA of one cell in your mother's womb.

¹⁴ In the light of even these few points about the cell, we ask: Since our parents did not consciously prepare the incredible genetic blueprint or the cell, who did? Can it reasonably be accounted for without an intelligent Designer?

¹⁵ Of all your organs, probably the most amazing is one that you will never see—your brain. It is made up of some 10,000,000,000 nerve cells, more than twice the number of people on the face of

How does the human brain give evidence of design? (15-17)

the earth. Each of these cells, in turn, may have thousands of connections with other nerve cells. The total number of connections is beyond imagination!

¹⁶ You have stored in your brain hundreds of millions of facts and images, but it is not merely a storehouse of facts. With it you can learn how to tie a knot, to speak a foreign language, to bake bread or to whistle. You can imagine—what your vacation will be like or how a juicy fruit will taste. You can analyze and create. You can also plan, appreciate, love and relate your thoughts to the past, present and future. The One who designed the brain obviously has wisdom far greater than that of any human, because scientists admit:

> "How these functions are carried out by this magnificently patterned, orderly and fantastically complex piece of machinery is quite obscure. . . . human beings may never solve all the separate individual puzzles the brain presents."—*Scientific American*.

¹⁷ In reflecting on whether there is a Creator who is the Supreme Being, do not overlook the rest of your body. Your eyes—more precise and adaptable than any camera. Your ears—able to detect a variety of sounds and to give you a sense of direction and balance. Your heart—a magnificent pump with capabilities that the best engineers have not been able to duplicate. Your tongue, digestive system and hands, to name a few more. An engineer hired to design and build a large computer reasoned:

> "If my computer required a designer, how much more so did that complex physio-chemical-biological machine which is my human body—which in turn is but an extremely minute part of the well-nigh infinite cosmos?"

WHO DESIGNED THE HUMAN BODY?

BRAIN: Far more than a computer, with capacity estimated at a billion times as much as used in present human lifetime.

EYE: A fully automatic, self-focusing, nonblurring color motion-picture camera.

HEART: A pump far more efficient than any machine devised by man. Pumps 1,500 gallons (5,700 L) or more daily.

LIVER: A chemical laboratory with more than 500 functions. Manufactures over 1,000 enzymes.

BONES: A structural frame weighing only 20 pounds (9 kg), yet strong as iron girders.

NERVOUS SYSTEM: A communications network that receives and/or acts on 100,000,000 sensations a second.

"FIRST CAUSE" OF THE UNIVERSE

[18] Some 3,000 years ago a Middle Eastern man named Elihu said: "Look up at the sky and then consider."*

[19] Have you done that on a clear, dark night? Everyone should. Only about 5,000 stars can be detected with the unaided eye. Our Milky Way galaxy, however, contains more than 100,000,000,000 stars. And how many galaxies are there? Astronomers say that there are thousands of millions—not of stars, but of galaxies, each with its billions of stars! How small humans are in relation to all of this! Where did it all come from?

[20] Scientists have discovered that the galaxies seem to be flying away from a central point. The theory of many astronomers is that thousands of millions of years ago, a tremendous explosion, a "big bang," started energy and matter spreading out to form the universe as we know it. Their theory does not explain what caused that to occur. But it does have an interesting implication, namely, that there was a beginning point, a moment when the universe was born.

"Today one can feel the scientific world tremble at the accumulating evidence for a 'big bang' origin of the universe. It raises the question of what came before, and scientists' most fundamental faith is shaken by being brought face to face with their inability to answer ultimate questions."—*The Wall Street Journal.*

[21] Yes, for persons who do not believe in God, there are puzzling questions: What or who put matter into the universe? Was the universe cre-

* Job 35:5, *New English Bible.*

What leads many persons to conclude that the universe was created by God? (18-24)

ated out of nothing? Since matter is considered a form of energy, what is the source of the energy?

ORDER FROM WHERE?

Dr. Paul Davies, lecturer in applied mathematics at King's College, London, writes in "New Scientist":

"Everywhere we look in the Universe, from the far flung galaxies to the deepest recesses of the atom, we encounter order. . . . If information and order always has a natural tendency to disappear, where did all the information that makes the world such a special place come from originally?"

Sir Bernard Lovell, of England's famed Jodrell Bank Observatory, writes that his feelings are the same as those of Albert Einstein:

"A rapturous amazement at the harmony of natural law, which reveals an intelligence of such superiority that, compared with it, all the systematic thinking and acting of human beings is an utterly insignificant reflection."—"Centre of Immensities."

---

[22] Dr. Robert Jastrow, director of NASA's Goddard Institute for Space Studies, observed: "In the face of such evidence, the idea that there is a God who created the universe is as scientifically plausible as many other ideas."

[23] Well-informed persons in every generation have concluded that there must be an intelligent

**How did
the universe
with its billions
of galaxies come to be?**

First Cause, a creator who is the Supreme Being. The Bible expresses how they felt, when it says: "The heavens are declaring the glory of God; and of the work of his hands the expanse is telling."*

²⁴ Whether you have yet concluded that God exists or not, what we have considered about life, about ourselves, and about the universe should help to explain why many thinking persons are convinced there is a God. That leads us to a related matter: If the Creator does exist, is it not logical that he would communicate with his creatures, and answer our questions: Why are we here? Why does wickedness abound? What does the future hold? How can we find happiness?

_____
* Psalm 19:1.

3

Where Can You Find Guidance?

WHAT stands between you and happiness? The problems you face? These may be of a personal nature—involving health, money, sex, your family. They may include the danger of crime, the shortages of life's necessities, job frustration, prejudice, the threat of war. Yes, most persons have problems that interfere with happiness.

² Despite efforts by the most educated and experienced humans, the problems continue and get worse. What was written long ago has proved to be true: 'The way of man is not in himself, it is not in man who walks to direct his steps.'* Is it not plain that we need guidance from a source wiser than man if we hope to find lasting happiness? But where is such guidance available?

³ Many persons believe that the universe is, in a sense, a 'book of creation' that testifies about a Creator. An ancient Hebrew king agreed, writing: "The heavens are declaring the glory of God." He also stated that the Creator has provided information in an actual written book that can 'make the inexperienced one wise' and joyful.†

---

* Jeremiah 10:23, *Revised Standard Version.*

† Psalm 19:1, 7, 8.

POINT FOR DISCUSSION: Why is it reasonable that God has provided a book of guidance? (1-5)

⁴ Since humans have the ability to communicate—even sending messages to earth from outer space—is it not logical that man's Creator could also? Moreover, since there are many things about the earth that give evidence of His interest in mankind, it is understandable that he would want to help humans. His doing so would agree with what we see in loving families: parents pass on knowledge and guidance to their children. But how would man's Creator do this for our benefit?

⁵ Writing has long been an excellent means for conveying information accurately and with much permanence. A written record is much less likely to contain errors than is a message widely spread only through word of mouth. Also, a book can be reproduced and translated so that persons using any language can read its message. Does it not seem reasonable that our Creator has used such a means to provide information?

⁶ More than any other religious writing the Bible has been viewed as a communication from our Creator, and for that reason it has had an extraordinary circulation.

What reasons are there to consider the Bible? (6-9)

Man's satellites can send messages to earth. Cannot the Creator do more?

Is it not logical that God would provide a book for mankind?

This is significant. If mankind's Creator were to provide a book containing his message for all men, we would expect it to be made widely available. The Bible is. It can be read in the languages of 97 percent of the world's population. No other religious book has been produced and distributed in so many hundreds of millions of copies.

⁷ Truly the Bible is the religious book for all mankind. Why? The writing of it began near the cradle of civilization. It is the only sacred book that traces the history of all mankind back to its beginning. Also, it tells of God's purpose to give opportunity for people of "all nations of the earth" to enjoy lasting blessings.—Genesis 22:18.

⁸ The *Encyclopædia Britannica* calls the Bible "the most influential collection of books in human history." It has had the widest influence and effect on history of any sacred writings. Hence, it is fair to say that no person can be viewed as completely educated if he has not read the Bible.

⁹ Yet some persons have avoided the Bible. Why? Often it is because of the conduct of people

and nations that *supposedly* follow the Bible. In certain lands it is said that the Bible is a book that leads to war, that it is a book of colonialism, or that it is a 'white man's book.' But these are mistaken views. The Bible was written in the Middle East. It does not approve of the colonial wars and greedy exploitation that have been carried on in the name of Christianity. To the contrary, in reading the Bible you will see that it strongly condemns selfish warring, immorality and the exploiting of others. The fault is with greedy people, not with the Bible. (James 4:1-3; 5:1-6) So do not let the misconduct of selfish people who live contrary to the Bible's counsel prevent your benefiting from its treasures.

WHAT WILL YOU FIND?

[10] Many are surprised when they first read the Bible. They find that it is not primarily a book about religious observances or creeds. Nor is it a collection of vague sayings or philosophies that have little meaning to the average person. It deals with real people who had concerns and problems like ours. Also, by presenting God's dealings with mankind in the past, it offers insight as to his will for us today. We encourage you to read Genesis, the opening book of the Bible. From the interesting accounts in it you will be able to learn much about God's purpose for all mankind. You will find lessons as to what can spoil a person's happiness. Also, you will learn about traits and actions that bring success and that please God.

[11] Some of the Bible's 66 individual books deal with the history and religious activities of ancient Israel. (Exodus, Joshua and First Samuel are a

---

What sort of information is found in the Bible? (10-13)

few examples you are sure to enjoy.) That history was written down so that we can benefit from it. (1 Corinthians 10:11) Hence, even though God is no longer directing one particular nation, nor expecting everyone to keep the laws he gave only for ancient Israel, we can learn much from such Bible books. And, as we will later see, what God did for the Israelites (as well as the animal sacrifices that they offered to him) has meaning for our lives.

[12] For a rounded-out view of the Bible, you should also read at least one of the accounts of the life of Jesus. The brief Gospel of Mark is a good example. After that, enjoy the exciting record of the founding of Christianity set out in the Acts of the Apostles. Then sample the Bible's practical counsel for Christians, as found in The Letter of James. Getting a basic taste of all the various parts of the Bible will help you to see why it has been so highly regarded over the centuries.

[13] If a few things you read in the Bible perplex you, be patient. It contains many deep things, as we would expect of a book provided by the Creator for mankind's study over the centuries. (2 Peter 3:15, 16) In time you will find answers to many questions, for the Bible accounts are interrelated. Questions that come up about one passage will be answered by other scriptures. The more you read the more helpful and satisfying you will find the Bible to be. Also, you will soon see that what the Bible says is very different from the teachings and practices of most churches. This will move you to want to read all the Scriptures, and you may find yourself returning to them again and again.

THE BIBLE—FROM WHAT SOURCE?

[14] You likely know persons who respect the Bible as literature or as ancient wisdom, but who feel that it is a product of men, not the Word of God. What are the facts?

[15] As you read the Bible you will see that various men did write down what it contains. Moses was the first, starting in 1513 B.C.E. The last man was Jesus' apostle John, writing near the end of the first century C.E. In all, some 40 men wrote the various Bible books. What sort of men were they? They were humble men, who were willing to expose both their own shortcomings and those of their nation. Their honesty is noteworthy, for they also said that they were writing what God told them to write. You can note examples of this at 2 Samuel 23:1, 2; Jeremiah 1:1, 2 and Ezekiel 13:1, 2. Should not this move us to consider seriously the Bible's assurance that "all Scripture is inspired of God and beneficial"? —2 Timothy 3:16; 2 Peter 1:20, 21.

[16] What the Bible writers penned is different in many respects from most ancient records. As any student of ancient history knows, the records from Egypt, Persia, Babylon and other ancient nations included mythology and gross exaggerations about the rulers and their exploits. The Bible, in contrast, is marked by truth and accuracy. It is filled with specific names and details that can be confirmed, even dated. For example, Daniel chapter five has information about a Babylonian ruler named Belshazzar. For a long time critics claimed that Belshazzar never existed, but was invented by Daniel. In recent years, however,

---

What evidence indicates whether the Bible is just from men? (14-19)

clay-tablet records have been unearthed and translated that agree with the details in Daniel's account. For this reason, Professor R. P. Dougherty (Yale University) wrote that the Bible is more accurate than other writings and proves that the book of Daniel was written when the Bible indicates it was.—*Nabonidus and Belshazzar.*

[17] If you travel to Jerusalem you can wade through an ancient water tunnel cut through solid rock. This lengthy tunnel was discovered and cleaned out only within the last century. Why is this of interest? Because it confirms what was recorded in the Bible more than 2,000 years ago about King Hezekiah's bringing water into Jerusalem.—2 Kings 20:20; 2 Chronicles 32:30.

[18] The above are just two of many examples proving the Bible to be historically and geographically trustworthy. But more than mere accuracy is involved, for some modern history books are accurate. The Bible contains things that could not be explained if it were a book of mere human origin. These have convinced many careful examiners that the Bible is from a Supreme Being.

HEZEKIAH'S TUNNEL

You can wade through this ancient water tunnel in Jerusalem. It confirms the Bible's accuracy.

[19] Though the Bible is not written as a science textbook, when it touches on scientific matters it is accurate and reflects knowledge that was not available to humans at the time it was written. For instance, Dr. Arno Penzias (1978 Nobel Prize winner) said about the origin of the universe:

> "My argument is that the best data we have are exactly what I would have predicted, had I had nothing to go on but the five books of Moses, the Psalms, the Bible as a whole."

Further, Genesis lists the progressive appearance of life forms in the very order now generally accepted by scientists. (Genesis 1:1-27) And, whereas other nations taught myths such as that the earth is supported by elephants or a giant, the Bible correctly indicates that it hangs upon nothing and that the earth is round. (Job 26:7; Isaiah 40:22) How did the Bible writers know things that have been "discovered" by scientists only in recent times? The information must have come from a source greater than themselves.

[20] There is something even more significant that sheds light on the Bible's origin. It is prophecy. Humans can guess about coming events, but they cannot consistently foretell the future with any degree of accuracy. (James 4:13, 14) Yet the Bible does. Long before Babylon became a world empire and desolated Jerusalem, God caused the prophet Isaiah to foretell that Babylon would be brought down in defeat. About two centuries in advance, God named Cyrus as Babylon's conqueror and told how the city would be captured. Isaiah also recorded precise details concerning Babylon's final desolation, when such calamity

What is significant about Bible comments on future events? (20-22)

was then more than 1,000 years in the future. (Isaiah 13:17-22; 44:24–45:3) It all came true. And so did the Bible's prophecies about Tyre and Nineveh. (Ezekiel 26:1-5; Zephaniah 2:13-15) You can visit ruins in the Middle East and see the proof for yourself.

21 Far in advance the Bible book of Daniel explicitly foretold other international developments. Babylon would be conquered by Medo-Persia, which, in turn, would be defeated by Greece. After Greece's prominent leader (Alexander the Great) would fall in death, four of his subordinates would take over rulership of the former empire. (Daniel 8:3-8, 20-22) That was long-range history written in advance, and it actually came about as foretold. How did Daniel know? The only satisfactory answer is stated in the Bible itself: "All Scripture is inspired of God." This concerns us, for as will be considered in a later chapter, the Bible has prophecies about things that have occurred in our time. Further, it describes vividly things that are still in the future.*

22 In addition to dealing with the future, the Bible helps us to cope successfully with the present. It explains why so much suffering exists, and it helps us to understand the purpose of life. It offers guidance from the Creator on how we personally can overcome problems and find the greatest happiness in life, now and in the future. Later chapters will consider some of the problems of life, as well as the Bible's realistic advice. First, however, we should get better acquainted with the One who has provided this advice.

* If you would like to study more about the Bible as a book of Divine authorship, please obtain the volume entitled "Is the Bible Really the Word of God?" published by the Watchtower Bible and Tract Society.

4

Learning About
What You Cannot See

MANY of the most fascinating things we cannot see. For example, because the marvel of a baby developing in the womb was long an unseen "miracle," the first photographs of it were most amazing.

² There are other important things that we cannot possibly see, such as the forces of magnetism and gravity. Yet they are real. We can learn much about them by observing the effects they produce. It is similar with God. However, if we are interested in learning about our Creator— which we should be—we have to apply ourselves. —Compare John 3:12.

³ Primarily, there are two means of learning about God, whom we cannot see. Paul, an apostle of Jesus Christ, mentioned one, writing: "His invisible qualities are clearly seen from the world's creation onward, because *they are perceived by the things made,* even his eternal power and Godship." (Romans 1:20) Yes, creation testifies about the existence of a Supreme Being. In addition, it gives indication of his qualities, what he is like. The second means is far more important, for it provides more exact information about God. It is the *written revelation* found in the Bible.

POINT FOR DISCUSSION: How is it possible to learn about an unseen God? (1-3)

WHAT IS HE LIKE?

⁴ As recorded in the Bible, Jesus said that "God is a Spirit." (John 4:24) That means that the Creator does not have a physical body of flesh as we do. This should not be difficult to accept for persons who are acquainted with such unseen realities as gravity, magnetism and radio waves. A major distinction with God, however, is that he is a living, intelligent Person with qualities that we can discern. What are some of these?

⁵ Have you ever watched huge waves crashing against a rocky coast? Or have you observed the tremendous force of a volcano? These are but small-scale indications of the *power* that the Creator must possess, for he made the earth and its forces.

⁶ With Einstein's famous equation $E=mc^2$, scientists explain that all matter is nothing more than energy locked up in the basic atoms. Men have shown this to be true with the explosion of their atomic bombs. Yet did you know that such tremendous explosions release less than one percent of the potential energy of the atoms? Imagine the awesome power of the Creator who put together *all* the atoms in the universe. Thousands of years before Einstein was born, the Scriptures acknowledged that the Supreme Being is the source of tremendous energy. (Isaiah 40:29) With good reason the Scriptures repeatedly call him "God Almighty."—Genesis 17:1; Revelation 11:17.

⁷ God has often used his power in ways that directly affected humans. An example is the Exodus, when God delivered Moses and the Israelites

Why can you be sure of God's awesome power and his ability to use it? (4-8)

out of Egypt. You may want to read aloud the brief account in Exodus 13:21–14:31. Picture yourself among those being protected by an awesome pillar of cloud by day and by a blazing pillar of fire at night. How would you have felt when it seemed that the pursuing army had you trapped against the Red Sea? Imagine, though, watching as God used his power to form the water into towering walls on both sides so you could escape. What a God he is!—Exodus 15:1, 2, 11; Daniel 4:35.

⁸ The Exodus also showed God's ability to accomplish things from a distance. To do this, he uses his invisible active force, his spirit, or holy spirit. Though this active force is impersonal, it can, like a powerful breath of air, exert power. God used his spirit in creating the material universe. (Psalm 33:6; Genesis 1:2) But he can also use it to strengthen and help persons.—Judges 14:5, 6; Psalm 143:10.

⁹ One who designs and then makes some machine certainly has *knowledge* of its structure and functions. Hence, does not what we see on earth and in the heavens assure us that God has vast knowledge? Chemists spend a lifetime seeking to understand the makeup of natural substances. What knowledge the One who created these substances must have! Also, scientists are studying the cell and minute forms of life. The Creator had to know these fields thoroughly in order to produce life in the first place!

¹⁰ God's knowledge extends over the whole range of the universe. He can call by name all the billions of stars that he created. (Isaiah 40:26)

What should we know about God as to knowledge? And wisdom? (9-11)

God's power parted the Red Sea

After just some of God's vast knowledge was recounted, a man named Job humbly confessed: "I have come to know that you are able to do all things, and there is no idea that is unattainable for you." (Job 42:2) Do we not have ample reason to feel similarly?

11 God is also the embodiment of *wisdom,* because he successfully applies his knowledge. For example, he designed plants so that they are able to combine water and carbon dioxide from air to form sugars and starches, which are needed as food for humans and animals. Plants can also make complex fats, proteins and vitamins that we use to keep healthy. All our food depends on an amazing cycle that involves the sun, rainfall, lightning and bacteria in the soil. (Jeremiah 10: 12; Isaiah 40:12-15) As a person learns of God's dealings, he comes to appreciate in his heart why one Bible writer exclaimed: "O the depth of God's riches and wisdom and knowledge!" (Romans 11:33) Is that not how you would want to feel about a God receiving your worship?

AN APPEALING PERSONALITY

12 It is easy to see that the Creator is a *considerate and an abundant provider.* We already mentioned some things about his arranging for food. But a writer of Bible psalms said:

"You set springs gushing in ravines, running down between the mountains, supplying water for wild animals, . . . You make fresh grass grow for cattle and those plants made use of by man, for them to get food from the soil: wine to make them cheerful, oil to make them happy and bread to make them strong."—Psalm 104:10-15, *Jerusalem Bible.*

How do you benefit from displays of God's personality? (12-14)

God prepared the earth in such a way that there can be more than enough food for all mankind. The tragic food shortages that cause so much suffering usually come from man's greed or mismanagement.

[13] Our Creator does more than abundantly supply what is needed to sustain life. He also makes it enjoyable. God could have provided nourishing food that was all tasteless. Instead, we have an endless variety of delightful flavors in healthful foods. Also, let us not overlook that God made us so that we can enjoy the beauty of colors, such as those of flowers and fruits. And he gave us the ability to enjoy the sound of music. How does all of this make you feel about God?

[14] Thinking on this, many persons have been moved to conclude that God must be *very loving*. They are convinced that he is. The Bible agrees, for the apostle John wrote: "God is love." (1 John 4:8) The Creator is the very personification of love; it is his dominant quality. If someone asked you what God is like, that would likely be your first reply. He lovingly expresses warm affection toward humans. God is no abstract idea nor a remote deity. He is a warm person with whom we can have a loving relationship. Jesus said that his followers could pray to God as their Father, someone close to them and interested in them. —Matthew 6:9.

[15] If you truly love someone, you want to see good come to that one. God feels that way toward humans. Out of love he warns us of things that would cause harm. These warnings are a protection. Also, they help us to understand God's stan-

How does God show his loving interest in you? How do you feel about this? (Psalm 30:4, 5) (15-17)

What do the sun, rain and productive soil indicate about God?

Is he not an abundant and a loving Provider?

dards and how he will act or react. For example, the Bible tells us that he hates lying. (Proverbs 6:16-19; 8:13; Zechariah 8:17) This assures us that God himself cannot lie; we can believe completely everything he says. (Titus 1:2; Hebrews 6:18) So when we encounter Bible statements that a person might view as restrictive, we should recognize them as reflecting God's loving, righteous personality and his interest in us.

[16] Further helping us to view God as a person to whom we can relate, the Bible shows that he has feelings in addition to love. For instance, he was "pained" when man rebelled against his righteous ways. (Psalm 78:8-12, 32, 41) He 'rejoices' when humans uphold what is right. (Proverbs 27:11; Luke 15:10) When we make mistakes, he is sympathetic, merciful and understanding. You will find it encouraging to read about this at Psalm 103:8-14. And the Creator is impartial, providing the sun and rain for all, and accepting worship from persons without regard for race or nationality.—Acts 14:16, 17; 10:34, 35.

[17] Happiness is something that most of us want. Thus we have reason to come to know the Most High. The Bible describes him as "the happy God" and it shows that he *wants* us to be happy. (1 Timothy 1:11; Deuteronomy 12:7) He is ever a rewarder of those showing faith in him. (Hebrews 11:6; 13:5) And God has made a way for humans to be healthy and happy endlessly, as we will discuss in later chapters.

"THE" GOD

[18] Another important thing that the Bible reveals about the Creator is that he has a personal

What can we know about God's name and life-span? (18, 19)

name. In Hebrew it was written with four consonants, like this: יהוה. Most modern languages have a common rendering of this distinctive name. In English it is Jehovah. Psalm 83:18 tells us that people should "know that you, whose name is Jehovah, you alone are the Most High over all the earth." (Compare John 17:6.) Note that he *alone* is the Most High. There is but one Supreme Being. The ancient Israelites often expressed it this way: "Jehovah our God is *one* Jehovah. And you must love Jehovah your God with all your heart and all your soul and all your vital force."—Deuteronomy 6:4, 5; compare John 17:3.

[19] Our God, Jehovah, is timeless, as reason would indicate. Scientists say that the universe is thousands of millions of years old. So the Creator of the universe obviously must already have existed before that. This agrees with the Bible's calling him the "King of eternity," without beginning or end. (1 Timothy 1:17; Revelation 4:11; 10:6) Man's few thousand years on earth are a brief moment compared to Jehovah's timelessness. —Psalm 90:2, 4.

OTHER BEINGS WE CANNOT SEE

[20] The Bible reveals that there are also created persons who are spirits. After the Almighty had existed alone for a long time, he chose to create other spirit persons. Initially, he produced "the firstborn of all creation" and "the beginning of the creation by God." (Colossians 1:15; Revelation 3:14) This firstborn was with the Almighty God in the beginning of creation. Jehovah would later use him also as a spokesman, or Word, in

Why is God not alone in heaven? (20, 21)

communicating with others. (John 1:1-3; Colossians 1:16, 17) Eventually, this firstborn Son was sent to earth to become a man. He is known as Jesus Christ.—Galatians 4:4; Luke 1:30-35.

²¹ Working through this first created Son, God made other spirit creatures, commonly known as angels. These serve God as messengers and perform duties in the universe, including services in behalf of humans.—2 Peter 2:11; Hebrews 2:6, 7; Psalm 34:7; 103:20.

²² Both logic and the Bible indicate that the firstborn Son who was both created and sent to earth by God would not be equal to his Father. Some persons who claim belief in the Bible teach that Jesus and his Father are equal parts of a composite deity. This is not a new idea, for many ancient religions worshiped groups of gods. But contrary to this, the Bible clearly says that Jesus, as a separate person, received power from his almighty Father. It assures us that the Almighty knew things that Jesus did not, and that neither when on earth nor afterward was Jesus Christ ever equal to his Father.—John 5:30; 8:28; 14: 10, 28; Mark 13:32.

²³ For thousands of years in heaven, the Son had a close relationship with Almighty God, so that he could learn from God and imitate his ways. Thus when a disciple asked, "show us the Father," Jesus replied: "He that has seen me has seen the Father also." (John 14:8, 9; 1:18) By our studying the Bible account of Jesus' earthly life we can learn much about the Father, such as why God does things and what he expects us to be like. Jesus once said: "I am the way and the

What is the relationship between the Father and the Son? (22, 23)

truth and the life." (John 14:6) It is vital for us
to come to know him better, and thus also to know
the Father. Reading the Gospel of John is an excellent aid. In doing so, do not concentrate on
mere facts or details, but try to absorb the spirit
of what Christ was like. He was the most important human you can learn about.

WE NEED GOD

[24] As we learn about the Almighty through our
observing creation and reading the Bible, it becomes evident that humans were not created to
live independent of him. We were created to have
a relationship with God, from whom we have
received life and whose daily provisions sustain
our lives. Trying to be independent of him and
his Word, the Bible, may be compared to a person's trying to find his way through an unknown
wilderness without a good map. In due course he
may get completely lost and die for lack of provisions to sustain life. It is similar when humans
omit God and his guidance from their lives. The
Bible and history assure us that to enjoy the best
life we need more than food, clothing and shelter.
For us to be truly happy, we need guidance and
help from our Maker.—Matthew 4:4; John 4:34.

[25] Many other persons know little about the
Creator. As you come in contact with such persons and as opportunity allows, why not pass on
some of the good things we have here considered?
It is a fine thing when persons are inclined to
share with others the important truths they have
come to know about Jehovah, our loving heavenly
Father.—Psalm 40:5.

Why should God be important in your life? (24, 25)

5

You Can Cope
with Life's Problems

"LIFE is full of problems," people say. You may agree.

[2] Money troubles plague many—bills, inflation, job insecurity, or finding decent housing. Serious marriage and family problems are common. Sex, alcohol or drugs are problems with many young persons. For the elderly, failing health brings difficulties. All these things give rise to damaging emotional tension or stress.

POINT FOR DISCUSSION: What reasons have we for optimism as to life's problems? How is God involved? (1-7)

INFLATION

SICKNESS

JOB INSECURITY

FAMILY PROBLEMS

HOUSING

³ How well are you coping with life's problems? News reports of widespread depression and of suicides clearly indicate that many persons just cannot cope. But there are millions who do not lose their balance when faced with adversity. Why?

⁴ These latter ones have learned to rely on the advice of mankind's Creator as found in the Bible. No psychologist, no marriage counselor, no writer of a newspaper advice column knows more about life than God does. He created the first humans, so he has a thorough knowledge of our physical, mental and emotional makeup. (Psalm 100:3; Genesis 1:27) Better than any short-lived human, Jehovah knows what is going on inside us and why we do the things we do.—1 Samuel 16:7.

⁵ Furthermore, he is better acquainted with the problems that confront us in this world than any of us are. Not for just a few years, but since the time of the first man, Jehovah has observed the problems of humankind—all of them. The Bible tells us: "From the heavens Jehovah has looked, he has seen all the sons of men. . . . He has gazed at all those dwelling on the earth. . . . He is considering all their works." (Psalm 33:13-15) That means that he knows what succeeds and what does not succeed in coping with whatever problems we have.

⁶ Generously, he makes it possible for us to benefit from his knowledge and experience. The Bible contains his counsel, set out in such a way that it fits our needs no matter what our circumstances in life, regardless of where we live. As Psalm 19:7-11 says: "The law of Jehovah is perfect, bringing back the soul. The reminder of

Jehovah is trustworthy, making the inexperienced one wise."

[7] Let us consider briefly how those reminders can help a person to cope with two serious personal problems, namely, severe stress and loneliness. After considering the Bible's practical help on these, we will examine other common problems —involving money, marriage and drugs.

HOW CAN YOU COPE WITH STRESS?

[8] Few people would say that they never experience severe stress. The more that our individual troubles grow—over money, the family, sex, crime—the more severe the stress becomes. A recent newspaper report commented that what best characterizes our times is not a way of acting or a style of dress. It is "the terrible feeling of tension."

[9] Did you know that stress can even shorten your life? Note:

"Dubbed the 'Twentieth Century Killer,' stress arises mainly from the psychological demands of contemporary life. The physical ills it generates now contribute to a vast number of hospital cases and deaths each year—at least tens of millions."—*To the Point,* African news magazine.

"Severe or prolonged stress can make the body more vulnerable to ailments ranging from skin rashes and the common cold to heart attacks and cancer."—*The Wall Street Journal,* U.S.A.

Even the unborn are affected. Stress on pregnant women, such as from marital discord or the fear of unemployment, can cause physical, mental and emotional damage to children in the womb.

[10] Stress also does damage in that it creates

How severe is the problem of stress? (8-11)

other problems. Because of it many lose work time, increasing their money troubles. It gives rise to violence, even in marriage. One husband wrote:

"Each day I get more uptight and nervous. I feel like lashing out at everybody and my wife usually gets it. I feel like getting stoned, but it doesn't do any good."

[11] Some stress is normal in life, and not necessarily bad. Getting out of bed in the morning involves stress, as does watching an exciting ball game. It is the severe, prolonged stress (or, distress) that is damaging. Of course, many of the pressures on us may seem unavoidable, involving other people or circumstances in our own life. Is there, nonetheless, something that we can do about harmful stress? If we could better cope with stress, it might lessen other problems, such as those affecting our health.

[12] A key to coping with stress was given by a man recognized world wide as one of the greatest teachers who ever lived, Jesus Christ. When asked which was the most vital of all of God's commands, Jesus replied, 'You must love Jehovah with all your heart, soul and mind. And you must love your neighbor as yourself.' (Matthew 22: 37-39) Apply that and you will be helped to cope with stress.

[13] For example, as you deal in a loving way with your mate or relatives, it is very likely that peace will increase. An atmosphere of warmth and happiness will develop. Tension will diminish. Yes, this Scriptural counsel can be followed with positive results in reducing stress.

How can Bible counsel help us to cope with stress? (12-14)

LIFE'S MOST 'STRESSFUL' SITUATIONS

RANK	LIFE EVENT
1	Death of spouse
2	Divorce
3	Marital separation
4	Jail term
5	Death of close family member
6	Personal injury or illness
7	Marriage
8	Fired at work
9	Marital reconciliation
10	Retirement
11	Change in health of family member
12	Pregnancy
13	Sex difficulties
14	Gain of new family member
15	Business readjustment

Based on research by Drs. T. Holmes and R. H. Rahne—"Modern Maturity."

[14] Nor is it limited to the family. As you apply the Bible's advice to show love—including the 'golden rule' of doing to others as you would like them to do to you—people will like you more. (Luke 6:31) That has proved true on the job, at school, in the community. Oh, there may be some friction, but certainly less. It is easy to see that, as a result, you will face less stress.

[15] Even in scientific circles it is being appreciated that what the Bible recommends will help persons to reduce stress and cope with it. Pro-

Scientists have found what about the Bible's counsel on love? (15, 16)

fessor Hans Selye (University of Montreal), one of the foremost authorities on the effects of stress, advised:

> "Rather than relying on drugs or other techniques, I think there's another, better way to handle stress, which involves taking a different attitude toward the various events in our lives."

He emphasized the need for a "philosophy of behavior by which people could live," which would "do much more for humanity in general than any discovery." What? After 40 years of studying stress, he said that the solution essentially came down to—love.

[16] Why is it that, even in day-to-day life, showing love as the Bible recommends is so practical? Why does it work? Dr. Selye said:

> "The two great emotions that cause the absence or presence of stress are love and hate. The Bible makes this point over and over again. The message is that if we don't somehow modify our built-in self-ishness, we arouse fear and hostility in other people. . . . The more we can persuade people to love us rather than hate us, the safer we are, and the less stress we have to endure."

[17] Anger is another cause of stress. We all get angry at times, as the Bible acknowledges. Yet it counsels: "He that is slow to anger is better than a mighty man, and he that is controlling his spirit than the one capturing a city." (Proverbs 16:32; Ephesians 4:26) So if we become angry, God's warning is to avoid flying into a fit of rage or 'blowing our top.' Often those who ignore that advice let out a burst of vicious words or get into violent fights. The results sometimes are physical

---

How else can the Bible's counsel help us with stress? (17, 18)

harm or ill will, with lasting stress. Hence, to the extent that you can follow the Bible's wise and practical advice about anger, you will be helped in coping with stress.

[18] As another example, the Bible also helps us to reduce stress by encouraging a varied and balanced life. Some persons are always frantically working, others seldom work. Some persons are always serious, others never. Any such extreme almost invariably causes problems and results in stress. However, read the comments in Ecclesiastes 3:1-8, where God says there is a time for every activity. You see, the Bible presents a realistic as well as a more balanced view of life. Work is good, as opposed to laziness. The Bible also urges people to relax some and enjoy the fruits of their labor. (Ecclesiastes 3:12, 13; 10:18; Proverbs 6:9-11) There is benefit to be gotten from some time spent in serious thought about what life means and how we should live it. Yet there is also value in relaxing with one's family and friends. To the extent that we can apply the Bible's counsel about balance, we will have less of a problem with stress.

COPING WITH THE AGONY OF LONELINESS

[19] "Loneliness is universal," said Toronto social worker Henry Regehr. "Stop anyone on the street and say 'tell me about your loneliness' and you will get story after story after story." In a poll of 52,000 persons, over 40 percent said that they *"often* feel lonely." It was the feeling that most consistently brought discomfort, spoiling happiness. Nor is it a respecter of persons, it strikes

How serious a problem is loneliness? (19, 20)

old and young, male and female. Though we might think of a single person, such as a widow, as the typical lonely one, some of the most desperately lonely are married persons who cannot communicate.

[20] Many persons try to block out loneliness with illicit sex, or to drown it with alcohol or to deaden it by compulsive eating. But the causes remain. One factor is the growth of large cities, where you can be surrounded by people yet feel extremely alone. The breakup of marriages has increased the problem. Even television seems to add to loneliness by cutting down conversation.

[21] What can be done to help to cope with loneliness? While not wanting to oversimplify the problem, it may be said that the Bible can help anyone to cope better with loneliness. Why is that? For one thing, loneliness often leads to depression and loss of self-respect. Cultivating a good relationship with one's Creator can help to restore such a person. He can develop a greater sense of worth, appreciating that God is interested in him, which can lead to a more positive view of life. (Matthew 18:10) Furthermore, the Bible outlines for Christians a way of life that can help to relieve loneliness.

[22] Lonely persons are often told to "keep busy." This has some value. But the Bible offers more realistic and practical advice. It urges Christians to be *active in doing good* for others, which also produces happiness. (Acts 20:35) We have an example in Dorcas, who spent time making things for other Christians, many of whom were widows. Her efforts helped them materially, and likely

---

What Bible counsel can help with loneliness? How? (21-23)

also helped them to overcome loneliness. At the same time Dorcas herself was not lonely but loved. You may enjoy reading about her in Acts 9:36-42.

[23] A very rewarding activity for many Christians has been that of helping others to learn about God and the Bible. In fact, the apostle Paul said that freedom to do that to a greater extent was an advantage single persons have, which, of course, would also help them to cope with loneliness. (1 Corinthians 7:32-35) Paul himself is an example of this. Read in Acts 17:1-14 how, despite unusual opposition, Paul kept occupied, helping many in the city of Thessalonica. Then note the resulting feeling of closeness between them, mentioned in 1 Thessalonians 2:8. Hundreds of thousands of Jehovah's Witnesses today can testify

Doing good for others, as Dorcas did, helps to prevent loneliness.

how rewarding it is to be busy teaching the Bible to others.

²⁴ Also, Jehovah's Witnesses regularly meet in groups to study the Scriptures. While learning, they are enjoying warm Christian fellowship. True, just being around other people is not itself the answer to loneliness, as many city people know. But those attending such meetings are

---

"In their own congregational life Witnesses form a genuine community of trust and acceptance. . . . The Jehovah's Witnesses offer [one] an alternative life strategy that gives its adherents a way to find identity and self-respect, a community of acceptance, and hope for the future."—"Religious Movements in Contemporary America."

---

among Christians who are striving to apply from the heart the Bible's encouragement to be genuinely interested in others. (Philippians 2:4) These meetings are stimulating, happy occasions. Those in attendance join in brief prayer to God, something that many have found helps them to realize that they are never alone. (John 16:32) We encourage you to attend a meeting of Jehovah's Witnesses. There you can observe how following Bible advice is helping many persons to cope with loneliness and other problems, such as those involving money or the family.

Of what value is Christian association? (Ecclesiastes 4:9, 10) (24)

6

Money Problems
—What Help?

"**F**EASTING makes you happy and wine cheers you up, but you can't have either without money."—Ecclesiastes 10:19, *Good News Bible*.

² Money is a major concern in every land. One reason is inflation. Every day it costs more to live. Many persons cannot even afford to buy the food they need. A growing number of men have to work at two jobs, and more wives go off to work. Families suffer. Health suffers. The money problems are usually compounded when credit buying comes into the picture. Relying on credit, many persons who are deeply in debt keep on spending for items they really do not need. This is true not only in advanced lands but also in areas where people have few resources.

³ What practical help does the Bible offer? Can it aid you to find or hold a job? Can it ease your family's worry about money, leading to a happier life?

DO HONESTY AND HARD WORK HELP?

⁴ "*People who work hard don't get a fair break. Do you agree?*" In a survey, 85 percent agreed.

POINT FOR DISCUSSION: Why is there need for help about money? (1-3)

The Bible offers what different and practical view of work? (Ecclesiastes 8:12, 13) (4-6)

It often seems as if success depends on cheating, stealing, bribery and influential connections. Yet the Scriptures stress the value of honesty and industriousness. For example, the Bible says:

"Let the stealer steal no more, but rather let him do hard work, doing with his hands what is good work."—Ephesians 4:28.

"The lazy man has longings, but gets nothing: the diligent man is amply supplied. You see a man skilful at his work? He shall enter the service of kings."—Proverbs 13:4; 22:29, Moffatt.

"Make it your aim to live a quiet life, to mind your own business, and to earn your own living, just as we told you before. In this way you will win the respect of those who are not believers, and you will not have to depend on anyone for what you need."—1 Thessalonians 4:11, 12, Good News Bible.

⁵ Both time and wide experience have proved that this advice is practical. Oh, it is true that some lazy persons seem to get ahead. But in general and in the long run, if you apply the Bible's counsel you are going to do better than those who ignore it.

⁶ Employers frequently complain that workers come in late, loaf a lot, are dirty and cannot be trusted. So a person who, following Bible principles, is punctual, careful, clean, trustworthy and diligent will usually find work. And he likely will earn more, for employers are often willing to pay for a well-done job. There are many reports from Jehovah's Witnesses of this happening.

⁷ But are not lying and cheating almost neces-

Of what value is honesty? (Romans 2:14, 15) (7, 8)

A SOUTH AMERICAN
BUSINESSWOMAN

In Georgetown, Guyana, 48-year-old Norma owned produce stalls at one of the largest markets. She cheated when weighing with her pan scales. If someone ordered 4 ounces of salt fish, she set the scales at 3, and so on. Also, the metal weights for the scales were short. Hence, her customers never got full measure.

One Sunday a relative gave her a copy of "The Watchtower" that discussed Bible principles in business. What it said about dishonest practices seemed to be speaking right to her. (Proverbs 20:23; Leviticus 19:35, 36) On Monday Norma threw out her false weights and got accurate ones. She began attending meetings at the Kingdom Hall of Jehovah's Witnesses and having a Bible study. Despite family ridicule, she became more convinced that she did the right thing.

How did it go with her business? She could not make a profit on some items without cheating, so she had to quit handling them. But with the remaining items customers saw a change and remarked, 'Since you became a Christian you are giving us more for our money.' As a result, business actually got better. Making an honest profit, Norma was able to pay off the mortgage on her home, put some money in the bank and make charitable contributions. And her health has improved, for she no longer gets the nervous headaches that she did when in fear of being caught cheating.

sary nowadays? Christians who, because of applying Bible principles, have refused to steal, lie or cheat have seen that Scriptural counsel works.

A Johannesburg, South Africa, firm that sold electrical appliances was not doing well. One reason was that many employees stole. One day the manager called the African staff together and fired them all. Yet the next morning an employee was on his usual train to work and met a fellow worker. 'How is it that you are going to work?' he asked. The other employee said that the manager had told him privately that, since he was honest, his case was an exception. The first man said that it was the same with him. On arriving at the job they met a third employee who also had been told privately to come to work as usual. All were true Christians.

Robert worked for a British road-building firm. One day a director said that if anyone called, Robert should explain that he was not in. Yet when Robert answered a call he explained that the director was occupied. Hearing that, the director criticized him. But the matter was dropped when Robert explained that as one of Jehovah's Witnesses he could not lie. (Ephesians 4:25) Later, when Robert was in line for a promotion, a greedy colleague tried to raise doubts about his honesty. Now the director spoke up about Robert's honesty. He got the promotion.

[8] Is honesty possible if you are in business for yourself? In some cases being honest may seem impractical. But it still is the best course. It helps you to have a clear conscience with God and peace of mind. Furthermore, many people prefer to do business with someone whom they feel will not cheat. It is just as the Bible says—you "win the respect of those who are not believers."

HELP WITH HOUSING

[9] Finding decent housing is another major problem. In some lands whole families are forced to

How can applying the Bible help with housing? (9-11)

live crammed into one room. Or, the difficulty may be to locate clean housing that one can afford. Can the Bible help with these problems?

¹⁰ When you rent (or lease) a home, you are dealing with someone else's property. It is noteworthy that God urged the Israelites to respect and care for others' property. (Deuteronomy 22: 1-4) He also encouraged physical cleanness. (Deuteronomy 23:12-14; Exodus 30:18-21) Accordingly, conscientious Christians try to avoid damaging property and they keep clean any home that they rent. For this reason, and because they 'live quietly,' they are widely appreciated as tenants and have found it easier to get housing.

A Christian family rented a house from the ex-mayor of one African capital. They kept his building clean and paid the rent on time. (Romans 13:8) When they were about to move away they introduced the owner to another family from the congregation. The owner mentioned that normally the rent "would be raised," which meant doubling it. But because he knew these Christians would be reliable, clean people, he left the rent the same, about half of what was charged for similar houses around there.

¹¹ Even when circumstances beyond a person's control prevent him from finding nicer housing, he still benefits. He will keep his home clean and neat. That makes for a healthier, happier life.

USING YOUR MONEY WISELY

¹² Wealthy King Solomon wrote: "Wisdom is for a protection the same as money is for a protection; but the advantage of knowledge is that wisdom itself preserves alive its owners."—Ecclesiastes 7:12.

What practical counsel is available about money? (12-16)

¹³ Solomon realized, as we must, that money provides a defense against the troubles that poverty can bring. So money is not to be wasted; it should be managed wisely. What practical counsel does the Bible offer us on managing our funds?

¹⁴ Jesus asked: "Who of you that wants to build a tower does not first sit down and calculate the expense, to see if he has enough to complete it? Otherwise, he might lay its foundation but not be able to finish it, and all the onlookers might start to ridicule him."—Luke 14:28-30.

¹⁵ That can be applied to family finances. Many couples have found it good to sit down and calmly calculate a budget to see if a major purchase is possible and wise. They have been further aided by the Bible reminder that unexpected events do occur. (Ecclesiastes 9:11) This has helped them to avoid impulse buying and long-term debts.

¹⁶ Also, note this insight: "The borrower is the slave of the lender." (Proverbs 22:7, *Revised Standard Version*) While the Bible does not forbid borrowing or lending, it alerts us that borrowing needlessly can, in effect, enslave a person to a bank or a lender. Wise is the person who remembers that in these days so many are tempted to buy on credit, only to wind up in debt, paying high interest.

¹⁷ The Bible has helped many families to ease money problems through cutting down on waste. Jesus set a fine example. After providing a meal for a large crowd, he directed that the leftovers be gathered. (John 6:10-13) Following such an example, old and young Christians can be more conscious about avoiding waste.

How have persons put Bible advice to good use? (17-19)

[18] Learning to apply Bible counsel about money may require a considerable change in viewpoint, but the results will be beneficial, as the following illustrates:

Soon after marrying, a young couple in Zimbabwe began having money problems. His wages were low; she wanted many new things and special foods. She also started working, but that did not seem to help much. The strain on their marriage was so great that it seemed questionable whether they would stay together. Some Christian elders offered to help. Using the Bible, they discussed the importance of a budget. (Luke 14:28-30) The couple saw the usefulness of preparing a shopping list with approximate prices and of buying foods for the whole week at a quantity saving. (Proverbs 31:14) The elders shared Scriptural counsel about contentment and the need

Bible counsel has helped
with the family budget

to avoid desiring luxuries that could not now be afforded. (Luke 12:22-31) What a help this Scriptural counsel was! Being more settled about money, the couple was happier. Even the neighbors commented on the improvement in their marriage.

[19] Those on a fixed income also have benefited from practical Bible advice. This was true of a retired couple in Spain:

Francisco and Maria's limited income simply is not enough. Yet they explain they get along fine by applying what they learn from the Scriptures. For example, Proverbs 6:6-8 says: 'Go to the ant. See its ways and become wise. It prepares its food even in the summer; it has gathered its food supplies even in the harvest.' Maria says that she learned to do this, buying things when they are readily available and therefore cheaper, such as fruit in season. She also waits for clearance sales to buy next year's clothing. They 'prepare their food in the summer' by cultivating a garden on a small piece of land that is a 45-minute walk from their home. The words at 1 John 2:16 also help. They have learned to be satisfied with home furnishings even if such are out of style. And rather than expensive entertainment, they enjoy helping others to learn about God.

AVOID HURTING YOUR POCKETBOOK

[20] Indulging in such practices as drug or alcohol abuse, smoking and gambling can drain your pocketbook. The Bible helps in these areas, too.*

[21] Consider liquor. The Bible does not prohibit the moderate use of alcoholic beverages. But it does advise:

"Pleasure-lovers stay poor, he will not grow rich who loves wine and good living."

"Do not be one of those forever tippling wine . . . for the drunkard and glutton impoverish them-

---

* See also Chapter 10, "Better Health and Longer Life—How?"

Why is Bible counsel about drinking of help? (20-22)

selves, and a drowsy head makes a wearer of rags."—*Proverbs 21:17; 23:20, 21,* Jerusalem Bible.

²² Heavy drinking hurts the pocketbook in various ways. Alcoholic beverages themselves are expensive, some persons spending up to half their weekly wage on liquor. In just the one Canadian province of Quebec over a billion dollars a year is spent on liquor. Another billion goes for things associated with heavy drinking—absenteeism from work and alcohol-related accidents.

In southern Chile a shoe salesman lost his job because of drunkenness. He then tried repairing shoes in a shed alongside the dilapidated house the family rented. Still, most of his money went for drink and his wife often had to get him from the jail. She also had to work late into the nights making wigs so they would have food money. But she began to study the Bible with Jehovah's Witnesses, which moved her to be a more understanding and supportive wife. This led her husband to sit in on the study. He learned that one cannot be a drunkard and a Christian, so he stopped drinking. The family then could eat better. In time they even bought a small home and a store where he carried on a successful shoe-repair business.

²³ What about gambling, whether large betting at a racetrack or a casino or the constant betting

How has gambling contributed to problems? (23-25)

"Eighty-seven per cent of Australians have taken part in some form of gambling over the last three months."—"The Sunday Mail" (Brisbane).

"We'd Rather Gamble than Eat! Queenslanders are spending an estimated $12 million a week on gambling—almost as much as they spend on groceries and meat."—"The Sunday Mail" (Brisbane).

with lottery tickets? Many persons have money problems because of compulsive gambling. They keep hoping to make a "big killing," but what they are really doing is squandering their funds, often with great hardship to their family.

How practical are Bible principles about drunkenness, smoking and gambling?

²⁴ An Australian man says that for years with him "gambling was an absolute obsession. I would gamble seven days a week, and more if there had been the days." He borrowed from friends until they avoided him. "Sometimes after losing I would bang my head on the wall and plead with my wife, 'Just give me 50 cents. I know I'll win.'"

²⁵ When he began to study the Bible, he was impressed with Jesus' counsel: "Keep your eyes open and guard against every sort of covetousness." (Luke 12:15; 1 Corinthians 6:9, 10) Concluding that his gambling reflected extreme greed, this man forced himself to quit. Being then able to use his pay to benefit his family, he could more fully appreciate the proverb: "Wealth got by scheming ["wealth from gambling," *Living Bible*] will diminish; but he who gathers little by little will increase his store."—Proverbs 13:11, *An American Translation*.

BEING CONTENT IS A KEY

²⁶ Concerning money, an area in which the Bible can provide some of the greatest help involves one's personal outlook. At 1 Timothy 6: 7-10 we read:

"What did we bring into the world? Nothing! What can we take out of the world? Nothing! So then, if we have food and clothes, that should be enough for us. But those who want to get rich fall into temptation and are caught in the trap of many foolish and harmful desires. . . . Some have been so eager to have [money] that they have wandered away from the faith and have

Why is Biblical advice on contentment useful? (26, 27)

broken their hearts with many sorrows."—Good News Bible.

[27] Whether they are poor or rich, those who love money are never satisfied. A hard-driving executive in California told his wife: "I want to become rich . . . and if I have to choose between you and [the company], you lose." He became head of a large corporation, a millionaire, and lives in a $700,000 home. Yet he says: "Whatever I have, it's not enough." The fact is that money does not assure happiness. Two years before he died, millionaire oilman J. P. Getty said: "Money doesn't necessarily have any connection with happiness. Maybe with unhappiness."

[28] The Bible, while not condemning the having of money or possessions, strongly warns against developing a love for them. It reminds us that life does not come from what we possess.—Luke 12:16-20.

[29] So rather than fill your life with anxiety by striving for wealth, be content with what you have or can reasonably obtain. Jesus' words at Luke 12:22-31 can aid us to have that view:

"Quit being anxious about your souls as to what you will eat or about your bodies as to what you will wear. For the soul is worth more than food and the body than clothing. Mark well that the ravens neither sow seed nor reap, and they have neither barn nor storehouse, and yet God feeds them. Of how much more worth are you than birds? . . . So quit seeking what you might eat and what you might drink, and quit being in anxious suspense; for all these are the things the nations

Jesus offered what sound counsel about wealth? (28-30)

*of the world are eagerly pursuing, but your Father
knows you need these things."*

³⁰ An expensive wardrobe, rich food and a luxurious house may give some pleasure, but they will not add a year to your life—they may take years from it. Yet you can find much happiness in life without riches.

³¹ Nor do you need wealth in order to have friends. Anyone who depends on his money to attract friends is making a mistake. "Friends" of that sort eat your food and share your possessions, but when the money runs out so do they. —Ecclesiastes 5:11; Proverbs 19:6.

³² But when you accept the Bible's balanced view regarding work, rejoicing in life and doing good things for others, you will have a "gift of God." As Ecclesiastes 3:12, 13 expresses it: "There is nothing better for them than to rejoice and to do good during one's life; and also that every man should eat and indeed drink and see good for all his hard work. It is the gift of God."

³³ So sound is God's counsel on these matters that a person might well wonder: Will God someday open the way for a complete end to poverty, undernourishment and poor housing, which are so often associated with money problems? *He will!* And later we will consider the evidence providing the basis for such conviction. But, first, let us look at some other problems that seriously affect people's lives now.

How can Scriptural counsel help you to have a richer life? (31-33)

7

Sex—Which Advice Really Works?

IF YOU were to take a poll on "What makes for happiness?" many of the answers would involve sex. That is to be expected, because sexual feelings and desires are a God-given part of every normal healthy person.

² Discussion of sex has become more open than in past generations. Also, sexual conduct has changed. More and more youths begin sexual intercourse at an early age, even in their early teens. Millions of couples, including many retired persons, live together and have sex relations without marriage. Among married persons, many have tried group sex, wife swapping or "open marriage," in which both mates agree to having sex outside of marriage.

³ Advice regarding these matters comes from a variety of sources. What is viewed as popular today has been encouraged or at least approved by many doctors, marriage counselors and clergymen. Some people get their ideas from "how-to" books or magazine articles. The thinking of others is molded by sex-education courses in school. Yet others simply pick up their ideas from novels, motion pictures and television shows that deal explicitly with sex.

POINT FOR DISCUSSION: What reason is there now to consider the Bible's advice about sex? (Proverbs 2:6-12) (1-4)

[4] As most persons realize, the Bible also discusses the subject. Many persons now tend to shy away from Bible standards, feeling that these are overly restrictive. But is this the case? Or could it be that applying the Bible's advice actually protects a person against much heartache and makes it possible to find greater happiness in life?

SEX BEFORE MARRIAGE—WHY NOT?

[5] Sexual desire and capacity normally awaken and grow during the teen-age years. So throughout history many young persons have had sexual intercourse before marriage. (Genesis 34:1-4) But in recent years premarital sex has become increasingly common. In some places it is almost the general rule. Why?

[6] One reason for the increase in premarital sex relates to the publicity given to sex in motion pictures and popular novels. Many young persons are curious, they 'want to see what it is like.' This, in turn, creates peer pressure and influences others to conform. As sex before marriage and sex without marriage have become widespread, many clergymen now say that it is permissible as long as the parties 'love each other.' More and more unmarried persons thus face the question, 'Why not have sex, especially if we use birth control?'

[7] Medical columnist Dr. Saul Kapel listed other reasons behind premarital sex, and made observations as to the effects:

'Sex is misused as a means of rebellion against parents. It is misused to attract attention, as a kind of "call for help." It is misused as a way of "proving"

Why has premarital sex increased? (5-7)

masculinity or femininity. It is misused as a social crutch in vain attempts to gain acceptance.

'When sex is thus misused, it never solves the problems that motivate it. Usually, it only obscures them.'

[8] No matter what the reason for premarital sex, no matter how common it is, no matter how many counselors and clergymen approve of it, the Bible advises:

"This is what God wills, . . . that you abstain from fornication; . . . that no one go to the point of harming and encroach upon the rights of" another.—1 Thessalonians 4:3-6.

Some may feel that God is here being needlessly restrictive. But do not forget that sex itself is a gift from Jehovah God; he is the One who created humans with reproductive powers. (Genesis 1:28) Is it not logical that the Author of human sexuality should be able to provide the best counsel on it, advice that can actually safeguard us against grief?

EFFECTS—PLEASURABLE OR PAINFUL?

[9] Sexual attraction and desire can, in the right setting, have fine effects. One, of course, is children. The first recorded instance of sexual relations says: "Now Adam had intercourse with Eve his wife and she became pregnant." (Genesis 4:1) In a family, resulting children can be a source of real happiness. What, though, if sex relations are engaged in by persons not yet married? The effect often is the same—pregnancy and children.

[10] Many who share in premarital sex relations

What is God's view of premarital sex? (8)
What effects come from premarital sex? (9-12)

feel that this need not be a serious concern. They have in mind available contraceptives. In some places teen-agers may obtain these even without their parents' learning of it. Nonetheless, teenage pregnancies abound even among sophisticated youths, who say, "It couldn't happen to me." News reports such as these prove it:

"More than one baby in every five born in New Zealand last year was born to an unmarried parent."

"Of every three British women under 20 reciting her marriage vows, one is already an expectant mother."

"One out of five teenage girls [in the U.S.A.] will become pregnant before she graduates from high school."

[11] This painful effect of sex before marriage has brought pressure on many young women and young men. Some seek abortion. Yet sensitive persons become severely disturbed at the thought of destroying a child that is developing within its mother. (Exodus 20:13) Feminine emotions and conscience are also involved. These are so powerful that many who have permitted an abortion have later regretted it deeply.—Romans 2:14, 15.

[12] Teen-age pregnancies bring greater risks to mother and child than do pregnancies of adult women. There is a greater risk of anemia, toxemia, abnormal bleeding, prolonged labor and forced delivery, as well as death during delivery. A baby born to a mother under age 16 is twice as likely to die in its first year. Illegitimate births also bring the parents many personal, social and economic problems. Furthermore, a child's security and development depend to a great extent on a stable home environment. Children deprived of that by illegitimacy may be seriously hurt for

life. Would you say, then, that the overall effects of premarital sex are pleasurable or painful? And is the Bible's advice, "Abstain from fornication," a wise protection?

[13] Ignoring the Bible's advice has also exposed many to another painful effect—disease. Women who began their sex life in their teens with multiple partners have a much higher rate of cervical cancer. There is, too, the very real danger of venereal disease. Some persons deceive themselves by thinking that gonorrhea and syphilis can easily be detected and cured. But experts of the U.N. World Health Organization report that some venereal disease strains now are resistant to antibiotics. Doctors worry, also, about the upsurge in genital herpes. It often harms children born to infected women. Yes, many young persons are learning to their sorrow the truthfulness of the Bible's warning:

"Every other sin that a man may commit is outside his body, but he that practices fornication is sinning against his own body."—1 Corinthians 6:18.

[14] Some think that premarital sex provides experience that can make for easier sexual adjustment in marriage. It is common in some lands for wealthy fathers to take their sons to prostitutes for "education." Persons may feel that this is helpful. But it really is not, according to our Creator, who has observed all human experience. Maintaining chastity beforehand lays a far better groundwork for a happy marriage. Canadian studies disclosed that teen-agers who had early pre-

What other reasons could you give for valuing Bible counsel on sex? (13, 14)

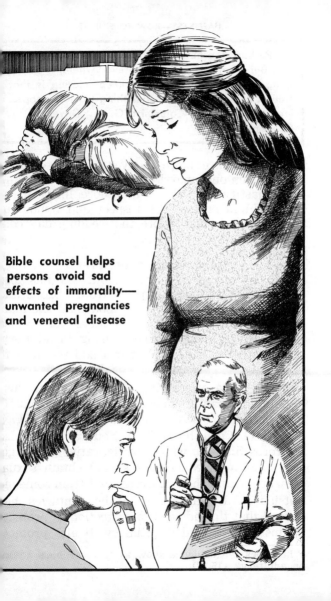

Bible counsel helps
persons avoid sad
effects of immorality—
unwanted pregnancies
and venereal disease

> "Perhaps the new 'sexual freedom' is 'liberating,'
> . . . But what I keep hearing, everywhere, is some-
> thing quite different. What I keep hearing is that
> free sex does indeed do something to most people.
> Free sex hurts."—Columnist G. A. Geyer, "The
> Oregonian."

marital sex are more likely to cheat on thei
mates when once married. But persons who main
tain chastity beforehand are more likely to b
chaste in marriage; the respect and honor fo
marriage they had before the wedding day con
tinue after it.

HOW ABOUT ADULTERY?

[15] Today's liberal counsel about sex has als
led to more adultery. Reports from Europe and
North America indicate that about half the mar
ried men cheat on their wives. More women als
are now approving of and sharing in adultery
often with the hope that it will add romance t
their lives.

[16] The Bible offers very clear advice on this
"Let the husband render *to his wife* her [sexual
due; but let the wife also do likewise *to her hus
band.*" (1 Corinthians 7:3) You can read als
Proverbs 5:15-20, which, in figurative language
says that married persons should obtain sexua
pleasure within their marriage, not from someon
outside it. Experience over the centuries ha
proved that this advice is a protection. It protect
against disease and illegitimacy. It also protect

What does the evidence show as to the Bible's advic
on adultery? (15-18)

against the hurt and sorrow that adultery often causes.

[17] When a man and a woman marry they commit themselves to each other. What happens when one of them breaks that trust by cheating? A study of extramarital affairs reports:

"There is tremendous guilt for going against one's word. Adultery is a personal crime, because you know precisely whom you are betraying or injuring."

This became clearer after many couples followed the advice about "open marriage," in which there was supposed to be agreement about having sex with other partners. In time the prime advocates of "open marriage" had to reverse themselves. The sad results forced them to conclude that "assurance of sexual fidelity is still an important and necessary attribute of most marriages."

[18] Adultery tends to produce jealousy and personal insecurity. God wisely advised about the harm these bring. (Proverbs 14:30; 27:4) Thus, though some persons feel they know better and that adultery is justified, the facts prove otherwise. Clinical psychologist Dr. Milton Matz frankly acknowledged:

"Most of us get clobbered by extra-marital sex when it occurs in our lives, whether we are participants or victims. . . .
"My experience with it has been that extramarital affairs are fantastically painful for everybody concerned. As a prescription for happiness, it doesn't work."

"Marital infidelity tends to create guilt, pain, and mistrust, while fidelity fosters security and deep joy."—Dr. C. B. Broderick, director of a marriage and family center.

SEX RELATIONS IN MARRIAGE

[19] Regarding sex, the Bible does not counsel u merely on what to avoid. It also gives us advic on what to do in a positive way that will con tribute to a rewarding life.

[20] Rather than presenting sex as a mere biologi function, the Scriptures properly show that it ca be a source of mutual pleasure for husband an wife. The Bible mentions being in "ecstasy" an 'intoxicated' with the sexual expressions of mar riage. (Proverbs 5:19) Such forthrightness help to dispel prudishness or shame regarding normal loving relations between husband and wife.

[21] The Creator counsels husbands: "Keep o loving your wives and do not be bitterly angr with them." (Colossians 3:19) For sexual rela tions to be truly rewarding, the couple must hav no barrier of bitterness or resentment betwee

What does the Bible offer about sex in marriage? (19 22)

them. Then marital relations can be enjoyed for what they really are, a way to express deep love, commitment and tenderness.

[22] Further, God urges husbands to dwell with their wives "according to knowledge." (1 Peter 3:7) A husband should accordingly take into account his wife's emotions and physical cycles. If, rather than being callously demanding, he is thoughtfully sensitive to her feelings and needs, it is likely that she will be more sensitive to his. This will result in mutual satisfaction.

[23] A common complaint is that some wives are cool or unresponsive. What may contribute to this is a husband who seems distant, silent or stern unless he desires intercourse. But do you not agree that wifely unresponsiveness would be less likely if a husband regularly were warm and close to his wife? It is more natural for a wife to respond to a husband who heeds the advice to clothe himself with "the tender affections of compassion, kindness, lowliness of mind, mildness, and long-suffering."—Colossians 3:12, 13.

[24] The Bible says: "There is more happiness in giving than there is in receiving." (Acts 20:35) That applies in many ways, and in principle it has been a realistic aid to sexual pleasure. How so? A wife's enjoyment of sexual relations depends largely on the heart and mind. In recent times much emphasis has been put on women's concentrating on their own bodily sensations and pleasure, but satisfaction still seems to elude many. However, Dr. Marie Robinson, who studied the matter, pointed out that when a wife cultivates respect for her husband and views intercourse as

How does applying this advice benefit a person? (23-26)

a means to 'give' rather than receive, she likely will find more satisfaction herself. This doctor commented:

"Gradually [the wife] finds herself allowing her new tenderness and concern for her husband to become a part of the meaning of her sexual embrace. She sees and feels the pleasure her sexual thawing brings him, and this process becomes circular, his increased pleasure giving her more pleasure."

So the Bible's counsel to be both giving and interested in others contributes to happiness, even in this intimate aspect of life.—Philippians 2:4.

[25] Heeding this counsel benefits us in another way too. Our viewpoint regarding sex, which includes the ability to transmit life, affects our relationship with God, who is the Life-Giver. Thus, avoiding fornication and adultery is wise, not only because it benefits us physically, mentally and emotionally, but also because these are "sin against God." (Genesis 39:9) And regarding faithfulness to one's marriage mate, Hebrews 13:4 states:

"Let marriage be honorable among all, and the marriage bed be without defilement, for God will judge fornicators and adulterers."

[26] When we consider how sex relates to a person's happiness, we need to look beyond today. With our lasting welfare in view, the Bible helps us to consider how what we do will affect both ourselves and others tomorrow, next year and throughout our life.

8

Family Life—
How You Can Have Success

BY FAR the majority of persons agree that family life and happiness are related. In one survey, 85 percent of the men said that they "feel that 'family life' is very important to a happy and satisfied life." Yet you may know of many men who have chosen to get divorced. More and more women, too, are opting for divorce to end marriages marked by boredom, conflict or oppression.

² We cannot change what others do. But we should be interested in improving our own family life, especially the relationship between husband and wife. We might all well ask: 'How is this relationship in my home?'

³ The Creator is the Originator of the family arrangement. (Ephesians 3:14, 15) He provides practical advice that has helped many, many couples to enjoy success in family life. That same advice can benefit you.

PRACTICAL LESSONS FROM THE FIRST MARRIAGE

⁴ In the opening portion of the Bible, we find

POINT FOR DISCUSSION: How can we work for more success in family life? (1-3)

What part did commitment play in the first marriage, and why is it vital? (4-6)

a record of how God began the first human family. Some time after Jehovah God had created the first man, Adam, He said:

" 'It is not good for the man to continue by himself. I am going to make a helper for him, as a complement of him.' And Jehovah God proceeded to build the rib that he had taken from the man into a woman and to bring her to the man. Then the man said: 'This is at last bone of my bones and flesh of my flesh. . . .' That is why a man will leave his father and his mother and he must stick to his wife and they must become one flesh." —Genesis 2:18, 22-24.

[5] Notice that the first family did not result from two persons just deciding to live together. God authorized the marriage and they were joined in a permanent union. Before the highest Authority in the universe, Adam accepted Eve to be his wife.

⁶ When a man and a woman take the steps required to form a valid and recognized marriage, they publicly *commit* themselves to each other. (Genesis 24:4, 34-67; Matthew 25:1-10) No such commitment is made when a couple simply lives together without benefit of marriage. Instead, their relationship is one that the Bible terms "fornication" or "adultery." (Hebrews 13:4) Even if they profess to love each other, their relationship will likely suffer in time because it lacks the firm commitment of marriage that the Bible shows to be crucial. For example:

A 34-year-old woman explains: "Maybe I'm old-fashioned, but the commitment of marriage makes me feel more secure. . . . I love the comfort of having admitted to ourselves and the world that we intend to stick together."

A 28-year-old teacher shared his realization: "After a couple of years, I began to feel as though I were living in a void. Living together [without marriage] provided no future orientation."

In a study of the matter, sociologist Nancy M. Clatworthy found that couples who made a commitment by getting married, but who had not lived together before marriage, expressed "a greater feeling of happiness and contentment."

⁷ The Bible account of the first marriage can also help us to avoid problems involving parents and in-laws. Such problems, according to one marriage counselor, are among the most common. Yet before there could be any problems with parents and in-laws, the Bible said of the first marriage: "A man will leave his father and his mother and he must stick to his wife."—Genesis 2:24.

What can we learn from the first marriage about parents and in-laws? (7-9)

⁸ Naturally, most of us love our parents. The Bible even encourages us to provide them with material aid in their later years, if it is needed. (1 Timothy 5:8; Deuteronomy 27:16; Proverbs 20:20) But the Scriptures emphasize that, upon marrying, your mate becomes your closest relative. Your husband or wife becomes the first one to love, care for and consult.

⁹ This view discourages a married person's 'running home' to parents if problems arise. And it helps parents to appreciate that, upon getting married, their children "leave" and form independent families, even if custom or finances require their living near or with the parents for a time. It is fitting for children to value and perhaps draw upon their parents' wisdom and experience. (Job 12:12; 32:6, 7) Yet what Genesis 2:24 says is a caution against parents' trying to direct or monitor the lives of their married children. Yes, applying this Bible counsel can contribute to marital success.

HOW MANY MATES?

¹⁰ We can also see from the Genesis record that God provided just *one* mate for Adam. In some cultures a man is permitted multiple wives. But does polygamy lead to family happiness? To the contrary, experience shows that it often leads to deep jealousy or rivalry, as well as the mistreatment of older wives. (Proverbs 27:4; Genesis 30:1) Both polygamy and the putting away of wives by divorce existed among the ancient Hebrews. God, while tolerating that, gave the Israelites laws to prevent gross abuses. In discussing the

---

What practical lesson can we learn from Genesis about the number of mates? (10, 11)

FAMILY LIFE—HOW YOU CAN HAVE SUCCESS   79

matter, though, Jesus directed attention to God's will as indicated in Genesis. When asked about divorce on various grounds, Jesus said:

"Did you not read that he who created them from the beginning made them male and female and said, 'For this reason a man will leave his father and his mother and will stick to his wife . . .'? . . . Therefore, what God has yoked together let no man put apart. . . . Moses [in God's law], out of regard for [the Hebrews'] hardheartedness, made the concession to you of divorcing your wives, but such has not been the case from the beginning. I say to you that whoever divorces his wife, except on the ground of fornication, and marries another commits adultery."—Matthew 19:3-9.

[11] Jesus made it clear that among his followers the standard would be, not polygamy, but having just one mate, as God had arranged in the beginning. (1 Timothy 3:2) Recognizing God's wisdom and authority in this regard is a step toward happiness.

[12] The same is true with what Jesus said about divorce. When it is possible to get a divorce easily, divorces abound. We see that today. But God considers marriage to be permanent. True, Jesus did say that if a person's mate is guilty of "fornication" (Greek, *porneia,* meaning gross sexual immorality), thus becoming "one flesh" with another person, the innocent party may get a divorce and remarry. Yet, otherwise, the Creator views a married couple as permanently united. Those who recognize God's authority in the matter thus have greater reason to work at strength-

The Bible encourages what view about divorce? (12, 13)

ening their marriage and overcoming any problems. (Ecclesiastes 4:11, 12; Romans 7:2, 3) Hence, rather than causing unhappiness, this view is an aid to achieving success in marriage. Experience shows that.

"During my married life," explains a man from the western United States, "I had acquired everything I wanted materially—a beautiful home, cars, boats and horses. Yet these things did not bring me happiness. My wife was not interested in the same things I was. We were always quarreling. I was smoking marijuana to find peace of mind.

"I spent most of my weekends away from home hunting. Also, my work took me away some. This led to a life of adultery. I didn't think my wife loved me, so I moved out and became involved with one woman after another until my life seemed at a dead end.

"During this time I read the Bible some. Ephesians chapter five convinced me to try again with my wife. I realized that she had not been submissive, nor had I taken a proper lead. But on a business trip the next week I again committed adultery."

A friend suggested that if he really was interested in God, Jehovah's Witnesses could help him. He continues: "The Witnesses did help. One of the overseers in the congregation spent time studying the Bible with me. Because of the big change in my way of life, my wife joined the study. Now for the first time our family life is a happy one, and even our two girls can see the difference. There are no words to describe the wonderful happiness that my wife and I have found in applying the Bible in our lives."

¹³ 'Still,' persons may feel, 'some marriages have serious problems, or the couple just does not get along.' What then? There are other practical things that we can learn from the Bible.

A HUSBAND WHO REALLY LOVES HIS WIFE

¹⁴ A key to family success is how a husband views and treats his wife. But who is to say which is the best way? What the Bible says about the first marriage again comes to our aid. The record explains that God used some of Adam's own body to produce a mate for him. The Bible later expanded on the matter:

"Husbands ought to be LOVING THEIR WIVES AS THEIR OWN BODIES. He who loves his wife loves himself, for no man ever hated his own flesh; but he feeds and cherishes it, as the Christ also does the congregation."

Then, after quoting Genesis 2:24, Paul continued: "Let each one of you individually so love his wife as he does himself."—Ephesians 5:28-33.

¹⁵ Some men may think that they should be harsh or remote in dealing with their wives. But the Author of marriage says that a husband should deeply love his wife and *show* that love. To be genuinely happy, a wife needs to feel sure that she is genuinely loved.

¹⁶ A husband's 'feeding and cherishing his wife as his own body' involves his striving to be a good provider. Yet he should not be so occupied with earning a living that he overlooks spending time with his wife and displaying warm interest in her as a person. Further, no sane man, even when irritated, is hateful or brutal to his own body.

How can husbands apply the Bible counsel for them? (14-16)

Hence, what the Bible says rules out a man's being violently angry with his wife.—Psalm 11:5; 37:8.

[17] The first woman was made to be 'a *complement* of her husband.' (Genesis 2:18) God recognized that the man and the woman had a different makeup. That is still true. Women usually differ from men in their qualities and ways. He may be decisive, she more humanly patient. She may like groups, he preferring solitude. He may stress punctuality, she being more "relaxed" about time. The Bible comment about God's creating Eve to be "a complement" should help husbands to understand such differences.

[18] The apostle Peter urges husbands to 'dwell with their wives according to knowledge, assigning them honor as to a weaker vessel.' (1 Peter 3:7) That "honor" includes accommodating the different tastes that a wife may have. A husband may like sports, but his wife may enjoy window-shopping or watching ballet. Her taste is just as valid as his. Honor allows for such differences.

[19] A wife's moods, affected by her cycles, may sometimes puzzle a husband, and maybe the wife too. But he can contribute to their mutual happiness by trying to understand and 'dwell with her according to knowledge.' Often what she needs most is to be tenderly held close while he converses with her in a loving way.

A WIFE WHO RESPECTS HER HUSBAND
[20] Since the wife must also do her part if there

What should a wife's being "a complement" mean for a husband? (17-19)

The Bible urges a wife to have what view of her husband? (20-22)

is to be a happy family, the Creator offers guidance for wives too.

²¹ Right after telling husbands to love their wives, the Bible adds: "On the other hand, the wife should have deep respect for her husband." (Ephesians 5:33) In the case of the first marriage, there were factors that naturally should have caused Eve to look up to her husband. Adam was created first. He had greater knowledge and experience in life, even having received directions from God.

²² But what about marriages today? If a husband sincerely tries to apply the Bible advice discussed earlier, this most likely will stimulate respect on the part of his wife. Even where a wife may excel in certain ways, or where her husband may fall short, there is reason to develop respect —out of regard for Jehovah's arrangement, of which the family is a part. The apostle Paul wrote:

"Let wives be in subjection to their husbands as to the Lord, because a husband is head of his wife as the Christ also is head of the congregation."—Ephesians 5:22, 23.

²³ This is not to say that the husband is to be a know-it-all tyrant in the family. That would be contrary to Christ's loving, considerate, understanding example. God urges wives to look to their husbands for leadership. On significant family matters husband and wife may consult together, like functioning parts of one body. Yet God holds the husband primarily accountable for the family.—Colossians 3:18, 19.

Why can wives trust that this counsel will help? (23, 24)

[24] Experience shows that what the Bible says on this subject is sound. As a wife works to merit her husband's love and care, and looks to him for guidance in family matters, she will often find that he more willingly shoulders his responsibility and discharges it in a loving way.—Proverbs 31:26-28; Titus 2:4, 5.

WORKING TOGETHER TOWARD FAMILY SUCCESS

[25] Communication is a vital element that is lacking in too many families. One social scientist observed: "Most married couples don't listen to each other, and many get into fights as a result." We are bound to have irritations, frustrations and disappointments in life. How can we prevent these from harming our marriage? Good communication helps. Be careful not to take it for granted, only to find that you gradually speak with each other less and less.

[26] *Work at* communicating. Do you really make it a practice to discuss your activities *and feelings?* Often we are in too much of a hurry to speak and we fail to hear what the other person is saying. (Proverbs 10:19, 20; James 1:19, 26) Rather than just biding time for a chance to speak, listen, try to understand, perhaps responding, 'Do you mean . . .?' or, 'Are you saying . . .?' (Proverbs 15:30, 31; 20:5; 21:28) A husband or a wife who sincerely listens to the thoughts and feelings of the other person will be less likely to act in a selfish or inflexible way.

[27] Communication becomes even more valuable if a couple will discuss mutual problems in the light of Bible counsel. For example, an excellent

What role does communication play in family success? (25-28)

Communication—vital for a happy marriage

groundwork for discussing family income and economic plans is found at 1 Timothy 6:6-10, 17-19 and Matthew 6:24-34. Much Scriptural advice about common aspects of family life is found in the book *Making Your Family Life Happy*.*

[28] Since the Bible's advice comes from the best authority on marriage and family life, Jehovah God, it stands to reason that, if we patiently and consistently apply it, its counsel can help us in working for success. Thousands of Christian couples around the globe have done this with happy results in their marriage.

---

* Published by the Watchtower Bible and Tract Society.

9

Youths—How Can YOU Be Happy?

YOUTH can be one of life's most exciting times. Your future is before you. So make the most of it. Pursue happiness.

[2] But that is not easy. Dr. Robert S. Brown made a study of young adults who, a few years ago, were determined to live up to their ideals for society and government. He reports that more than a third of them became disillusioned, depressed and anxious.

[3] You often hear it said that getting a good education is the answer. But today many young persons who do so still have trouble finding employment. Others who make out well financially discover that their high-paying jobs leave their role in life unfulfilled. Nor do most youthful romances lead to happiness. In some places, 80 percent of teen-age marriages fail within five years.

[4] What can you do so that it will be different with you, so that you will really enjoy yourself now and have a satisfying future? Or, if you are a parent, how can you help your offspring to achieve that goal?

TAKING THE CREATOR INTO CONSIDERATION

[5] Often young persons are influenced by others

POINT FOR DISCUSSION: Why is happiness a challenge for young persons? (1-4)

Why should you take God into consideration? (5-8)

of their age, who have limited experience in life. The Bible observes:

"Shrewd is the one that has seen the calamity and proceeds to conceal himself, but the inexperienced have passed along and must suffer the penalty." —Proverbs 22:3; 13:20.

A young person who is realistic will admit that few of his schoolmates or friends are deeply concerned about *his* lasting welfare. You could ask, In the years to come, will they then care if my happiness is spoiled by what I do now?'

⁶ But who does care and can offer you the best advice? Your Creator. He wants youths to enjoy life. He is not negative about all that appeals to young hearts and eyes. While he does not shield youths from the bitter results of a reckless course, he does what you would expect of someone truly interested in you: He warns you about things that will bring grief and calamity, and he offers advice on how to avoid these pitfalls. (Proverbs 27:5; Psalm 119:9) The Scriptures say in this regard:

"Rejoice, young man, in your youth, and let your heart do you good in the days of your young manhood, and walk in the ways of your heart and in the things seen by your eyes. But know that on account of all these the true God will bring you into judgment. So remove vexation from your heart, and ward off calamity from your flesh."—Ecclesiastes 11:9, 10.

⁷ There is, though, more reason to take the Creator into consideration than his being interested in you. As you likely have noted, many young persons drift rather aimlessly in life. They have no particular goal nor any firm standards on which to base their life. Often they turn to drugs, smoking and dangerous thrills to fill the emptiness in their life or to find some excitement

in an otherwise dull life. You may even have done some of those things, whether aware of the hazards or not. Are you satisfied with your life up till now and with what you see in the future? Is it not time to pause and think about your life?

[8] As we considered earlier, for a person's life to have meaning and to be in harmony with the facts, he must recognize that there is a Creator of the universe. That One, our Maker, has standards. (Psalm 100:3) Those standards are in line with how he made us to live. They are practical and conducive to happiness. We saw evidence of that in earlier chapters where premarital sex, heavy drinking and gambling were discussed.* So if you want a pleasant life, would it not be wise to take the Creator into consideration when you think about how you will live, what standards you will uphold and where your life is heading?

LIFE WITH PURPOSE AND SELF-RESPECT

[9] We noted in Ecclesiastes 11:9, 10 some Bible comments directed to youth. That book of the Bible concludes:

> "The conclusion of the matter, everything having been heard, is: Fear the true God and keep his commandments. For this is the whole obligation of man."—Ecclesiastes 12:13.

[10] Earth wide there are hundreds of thousands of young persons who have given serious thought to their lives. They have considered the Creator and studied his Word. And they have seen

---

* Music, dating, clothing, sports, school and other concerns of young persons are discussed in the light of the Bible in the book *Your Youth—Getting the Best out of It,* published by the Watchtower Bible and Tract Society.

Why is it natural for you to be concerned about God's will? (Psalm 128:1, 2) (9, 10)

that one of the basic requirements for happiness is to live in harmony with their Maker. That should also be your duty and purpose in life. Living the way the Scriptures outline is not odd, extreme or unpleasant. Rather, it is a balanced

FINDING PURPOSE IN LIFE

A department of the Office of the Prime Minister of Japan took a survey in various lands. It examined what young persons' views are about life's purpose and the future. Studying the results, Professor San-shiro Shirakashi concluded that "the world's youth have a pessimistic attitude" about the future, which affects their conduct and general outlook on life. But that can change.

A student named Linda relates: "From my studies in college, I could see that the life-style I was raised with was vanishing. Conditions all over the world were worsening, and I had no answers and no idea where to turn for answers."

While she was home in California on vacation two of Jehovah's Witnesses called at her door. She says: "They told me that the answers were to be found in the Bible. We discussed the paradise earth that God will establish under his new order and his promise to eliminate the wicked. I had never been taught that such wonderful truths were to be found in the Bible."

After Linda returned to Arizona, she contacted the local congregation of Jehovah's Witnesses and accepted the offer of a free weekly Bible study. That helped her to learn standards that gave her life stability. Also, she gained purpose in life, so that today her life is much happier and more re-warding.

and meaningful way of life. It enables a person
to deal wisely and successfully with questions
about money, employment, morals, family life,
recreation and other matters that you now face
or will yet face. The experience of Jehovah's Witnesses confirms that wisdom based on the Scriptures

"is a tree of life to those taking hold of it, and
those keeping fast hold of it are to be called happy."
—Proverbs 3:18.

The Bible counsels: "My son, do not forget my
teaching, let your heart keep my principles, for
these will give you lengthier days, longer years of
life, and greater happiness."—Proverbs 3:1, 2, *Jerusalem Bible*.

¹¹ When you follow the Bible's advice, you may
stand out as somewhat different from the average
youth. In fact, a few persons might chide you
about this. (1 Peter 2:20; 4:4) Would you let that
hold you back from a course that will make your
life more pleasant?

¹² There are many youths who talk about thinking for themselves, yet the facts show that they
are afraid to be different. The Bible, though, contains fine examples of young persons who did not
follow the crowd. While being normal youths, with
interests, concerns and hopes just as you have,
they guided their thinking and actions by God's
wise counsel.

¹³ You can read one example in Daniel 1:6-20;
3:1-30. Three young Hebrew companions of Daniel
were willing to be different from the majority
around them. When they were ordered to bow to
an image, something God's Word forbade, they
refused. Would you have been able to do that?

If living with God in mind makes you different, is that
bad? (11-14)

Others even wanted to kill them for their stand. Yet they stuck to their principles, and you will see from the account that God approved of and protected them. In the end, the king of Babylon honored them, confirming what Solomon wrote: "I am also aware that it will turn out well with those fearing the true God."—Ecclesiastes 8:12; Exodus 20:4, 5.

¹⁴ Those young men gained the respect of others, but they had self-respect also. The same has been true of many youthful Witnesses of Jehovah in modern times. Schoolmates have expressed admiration for their convictions and the fact that these Christians know where they are heading in life. Do you not agree that being respected and having self-respect make life more meaningful?

FAMILY HAPPINESS

¹⁵ Bible counsel also contributes to more rewarding lives for young persons by making for closer family ties.

¹⁶ You no doubt know of families where a chasm exists between the parents and the children, whether these are very young or are teen-agers. Often this gap develops when parents try to direct their offspring, who resent being told what to do or what not to do.

¹⁷ The Bible helps overcome this problem by offering balanced guidance to both youths and parents, such as:

"Children, it is your Christian duty to obey your parents, for this is the right thing to do. 'Respect your father and mother' is the first commandment that has a promise added: 'so that all may go well with you, and you may live a long time in the land.'

What reasons do you have to follow the Scriptures in your family? (15-20)

Who cared for you when you were sick?

Parents, do not treat your children in such a way as to make them angry. Instead, raise them with Christian discipline and instruction."—Ephesians 6:1-4, *Good News Bible*.

¹⁸ Of course, no parents are perfect. Still it is "the right thing" for young persons to respect their parents. Why? In part, because our parents have done so much for us—feeding us, caring for us when we were sick, working to provide a home and to fill our needs. We could not have hired anyone to do all that they have done and with the loving interest they have shown. So it is morally right to respect them, even as we would like to receive respect from children that someday we might have.

¹⁹ Youths who sincerely try to apply such Bible advice are going to feel more secure. They will be contributing to a closer family, which will make their life more peaceful and happy. And they will be protected from some problems that parents can foresee because of their greater experience in life. (Proverbs 30:17) Nor to be overlooked is the satisfaction the young persons can gain from knowing that they are acting in accord with their Creator's will.

²⁰ Accepting Biblical counsel benefits young persons in other ways, too. By appreciating the value of cooperation and of having respect for authority, they are better able to function smoothly at school, in later employer-employee relations and when dealing with officials. (Matthew 5:41) Also, taking Bible counsel to heart will make for happiness when they have mates and children of their own.

PARENTS PLAY A VITAL ROLE

²¹ In giving attention to how young persons can be happy, we cannot ignore the vital role that parents play. Most parents sense their respon-

How can parents help their children follow a wise course? (21)

Studying God's Word helps youths to find happiness

sibility to try to provide good food, clothing and a pleasant home for their children. But if youths are to become fine persons, they will need parental instruction, correction and moral guidance. The Bible has proved to be the finest basis for this. (Matthew 11:19) Deuteronomy 6:6, 7 explains that such instruction should be a regular part of family life, not something mentioned just once in a while. Also, this instruction can, *and should,* begin at an early age.—2 Timothy 3:15; Mark 10:13-16.

[22] Few parents with young children would be surprised to read: "Foolishness is tied up with the heart of a boy [or, girl]; the rod of discipline is what will remove it far from him." (Proverbs 22:15) But what does that mean? Some parents are so severe that they physically harm their children with beatings. Others claim that children should be allowed to develop on their own. Neither extreme is correct.

[23] We read earlier that parents are to 'raise their children with Christian discipline and instruction.' (Ephesians 6:4, *Good News Bible*) Brutality is not Christian discipline. (Proverbs 16:32; 25:28) Loving discipline may be expressed with a firm word. That is particularly so if parents make clear the reason for their rule and if they consistently stand behind what they say. When foolishness in a youth's heart still moves him or her to disobey —and that often occurs—some form of punishment will impress the idea. Taking away a privilege may work. God's Word says, though, that in some cases physical chastisement—spanking, given without wrath—may be needed.—Proverbs 23:13, 14; 13:24.

What sort of discipline should parents provide? (22-24)

[24] As small children grow older, the way of dealing with them will change. Whereas a spanking may have worked best with a young boy, as he gets older other methods may be better and more appropriate. Similarly, parents should gradually permit a son or a daughter more freedom of action and responsibility.—1 Corinthians 13:11.

[25] Love for your children is vital in order to help them with their problems. It should be the motive behind discipline, and it makes correction easier to take. Failure to provide guidance and discipline for one's children is like denying one's parenthood of them. This is explained at Hebrews 12:5-11, which points out that Jehovah himself gives discipline out of love.

[26] Love for God is also important. This will move parents to hate things that God condemns, such as lying, greediness, stealing, homosexuality and fornication. (1 Corinthians 6:9, 10; Psalm 97:10) Parents who thus show their love for God will set a proper example for children, which is important. Combined with this, parents should cultivate in their children the same hatred for what is bad as well as love for God and for what is fine.

[27] Since the family is a young person's primary world, parents should work to make that secure. It has been said that one of the greatest things a father can do for his children is to love their mother. When homelife is based on love and Christian wisdom, young persons will have a firm foundation on which to stand. They will have sound standards and will be helped to consider their Creator from youth onward.—Ecclesiastes 12:1, 13, 14.

How will family love affect youth problems? (25-27)

10

Better Health and Longer Life—How?

GOOD health can contribute much to a person's happiness. Yet all of us get sick at times. And serious illness can lead to death. These problems are considered in the Bible, which provides guidelines that can aid a person to enjoy better health and longer life.

² The Scriptures remind us that Jehovah God is the Source of life. Because of him "we have life and move and exist." (Psalm 36:9; Acts 17:25, 28) And he tells us much about how to look after ourselves. There are costly and crippling diseases that can be avoided by paying attention to the counsel in his Word. Those who have done so have reason to agree with the Bible writer who said: "The law of [God's] mouth is good for me, more so than thousands of pieces of gold and silver."—Psalm 119:72; 73:28; Proverbs 4:20-22.

COUNSEL THAT PROMOTES GOOD HEALTH

³ The Bible is not primarily a guidebook on health. But it contains counsel that promotes good health. That can be clearly seen from God's regulations for the nation of Israel. Here are some examples: Long before the practice of modern medicine, God's law to Israel required that a

---

POINT FOR DISCUSSION: What reasons do you have to know that God is interested in your health? (1-6)

person who had, or seemed to have, a contagious disease be quarantined. (Leviticus 13:1-5) Excrement was to be disposed of away from human habitations, thus preventing the spread of disease or the contamination of water. (Deuteronomy 23:12-14) If garments or vessels contacted an animal that had died of itself (perhaps from disease), they were to be either washed before reuse or destroyed. (Leviticus 11:27, 28, 32, 33) Israelite priests were to wash before serving at the altar, thus taking the lead in cleanliness. —Exodus 30:18-21.

⁴ Medical men have since learned the practical value of such measures, which can still be applied with benefit: Minimizing contact with others when you or they seem to have an illness that might be contagious. Taking care not to contam-

Cleanliness is an aid to good health

inate drinking water or food with human wastes or garbage. Keeping cooking and eating utensils clean. Caring for personal hygiene by regular bathing, also by washing one's hands after using the toilet.

⁵ Venereal diseases are usually contracted by immoral conduct, which God condemns. (Hebrews 13:4; Ephesians 5:

5) But by being chaste before marriage and restricting sexual relations to one's mate after marriage, Christians are protected against these dreadful diseases.

⁶ Also, better health can come from applying Scriptural counsel concerning a person's general way of life. For example, the Bible commends hard work. It says that the man who puts in a good day's work will sleep better. And it speaks highly of finding enjoyment in the food and drink you can get from your labor, while avoiding gluttonous overindulgence. Do you not agree that if you work hard, get enough sleep, enjoy your meals and are "moderate in habits," you will be healthier and happier?—Ecclesiastes 2:24; 5:12; 9:7-9; Ephesians 4:28; 1 Timothy 3:2, 11.

TOBACCO, ALCOHOL AND DRUGS

⁷ Dr. Joel Posner reports that in the United States, for example, 60 percent of the money spent for health care is for illnesses related to the use of tobacco and alcohol. How is the Bible helpful in this regard?

⁸ Consistent with God's advice on cleanliness or purity, the apostle Paul wrote to Christians: "Dear friends, let us purify ourselves from everything that pollutes either body or spirit." (2 Corinthians 7:1, *Twentieth Century New Testament*) Many persons have seen that using tobacco conflicts with that counsel. Drawing smoke into the lungs is unnatural. It pollutes the body and shortens a person's life expectancy. Studies have established that smokers have more heart disease, lung cancer, hypertension and fatal pneumonia.

⁹ Also, consider the effects on persons around

What Bible counsel bears on the use of tobacco? (7-9)

"There is now added evidence that cigarette smoke harms not only the user but those around him. . . . If you smoke you should consider the effect both physically and psychologically on your child as well as yourself. Your own smoking is hazardous to the health of your child."—Medical columnist Dr. Saul Kapel.

the smoker—his family and associates. Jesus Christ said that the second commandment in God's law given to Israel was: "You must love your neighbor as yourself." (Mark 12:31) Is that not what you want to do? But what are the effects of smoking? It harms the user and it injures the health of others who breathe the smoke.

¹⁰ What about using alcoholic beverages? Many persons find them tasty and relaxing. The Bible does not forbid beverages that contain alcohol, which the body can "burn" as fuel or food. (Psalm 104:15; Ecclesiastes 9:7) But it does warn: "Wine is a ridiculer, intoxicating liquor is boisterous, and everyone going astray by it is not wise." (Proverbs 20:1) And the Bible pointedly condemns drunkenness. (1 Corinthians 6:9, 10; 1 Peter 4:3) Anyone who drinks too much too often definitely is "not wise," as the scriptures say. In time, such a person may ruin his liver, with serious, or even fatal consequences. The stomach may be damaged. The abuser of alcohol can become disposed to heart attacks and strokes. Both his memory and his muscle coordination may be impaired, too.

¹¹ The Bible counsel on drunkenness is also helpful regarding drugs such as heroin, cocaine, betel

---

How does the Bible help us in our view of alcohol? Of drugs? (10, 11)

nut, marijuana and LSD. These are widely used, not for "food" or medical purposes, but solely to bring an intoxicating "high," hallucinations or an escape from reality. Such drugs may not have been used in Bible times. Yet the Bible speaks out strongly against drunkenness and the "debauchery" associated with it. Would not that same counsel apply to anything else that might cause one to become intoxicated and act in an unrestrained or debauched manner? (Ephesians 5:18) Often persons under the influence of drugs injure themselves or are hurt by others. (Compare Proverbs 23:29, 35.) These drugs are also linked to other health dangers, including lung disease, brain and genetic damage, malnutrition and hepatitis. So applying the counsel found in the Bible definitely can result in health benefits.

"Research links marijuana to many potentially serious health problems. They include lung damage and possibly cancer, mental and neurological disturbances, defects in the body's ability to fight disease, impaired sexual performance and the threat of chromosome damage and birth defects."
—"Newsweek."

WHY AND HOW TO APPLY GOD'S COUNSEL

12 The prospect of being healthier and living longer appeals to all sane persons. That is one good reason for accepting and applying the Scriptural counsel we have considered. (Psalm 16:11) But is that reason sufficient? You likely know persons who will accept risks because of the pleasure or thrill they hope to get. It should be different, though, with persons who have faith in God and who recognize that he has revealed himself through the Bible. Since our life is from him, we should be concerned with using it in harmony with the guidance he offers in the Bible. We would be ungrateful if we were to accept life from Jehovah and then deliberately ignore his wise and loving counsel on how to use our life.

13 Furthermore, as the Giver of life, does not God have the *right* to direct how we should live? He is the Ultimate Authority in the universe. The Bible writer James called him the 'One who is lawgiver and judge.' (James 4:12; compare Isaiah 45:9.) Hence, with regard to personal habits, we ought to be moved to apply what God says *because He says it.*

What reasons do you have for applying God's counsel in your life? What aid is available? (12-16)

[14] This outlook has provided a powerful motivation for many persons who long were unsuccessful in ending a harmful addiction. What they were doing became more serious when they saw that they needed to change, not just for the sake of their health, but because it was in accord with God's will. Jesus told his followers that the greatest command is to love Jehovah "with your whole heart and with your whole soul and with your whole mind." (Matthew 22:37) To do that, a person must break free from things that drug and damage the mind or that pollute the body.

[15] An added help is to associate with persons who are endeavoring to live in accord with God's counsel. The apostle Peter wrote that some, before becoming Christians, had "proceeded in deeds of loose conduct, lusts, excesses with wine, revelries, drinking matches, and illegal idolatries." (1 Peter 4:3) As they worked to change, they could be strengthened by meeting with fellow Christians. They would thus be encouraged to study and apply God's Word. And if, while making the needed changes, they weakened or felt extra strain, they could get help. How? By visiting and speaking with mature Christians, who would be sympathetic, understanding and upbuilding.—Ecclesiastes 4:9, 10; Job 16:5.

[16] If you would like such assistance, you are welcome to attend the meetings of Jehovah's Witnesses. Experienced Christians there will be happy to help you to learn and apply Bible counsel. As you make progress in doing so, you will have the satisfaction of knowing that you are striving to please your Creator. And you will be on the road to better health and longer life, with happiness.

11

Sickness and Death
—Why?

NO MATTER what people may do to care for their health, they grow older, get sick and finally die. No one can avoid it. Even men devoted to God could not. (1 Kings 1:1; 2:1, 10; 1 Timothy 5:23) Why is it that way?

2 Our body cells seem to have the potential for replacing worn-out ones far longer than they now do, and our brain has more capacity than we could use in many life-spans. Why—if we are not meant to use these capacities? Actually, scientists cannot explain why we grow old, get sick and die. But the Bible does.

THE CAUSE OF SICKNESS AND DEATH

3 The apostle Paul points us in the right direction, saying: "In Adam all are dying." (1 Corin-

POINT FOR DISCUSSION: Why are sickness and death a puzzle? (1, 2)

How did sickness and death come to affect us? (3-5)

Science writer Isaac Asimov explained that the RNA molecules in the human brain provide "a filing system perfectly capable of handling any load of learning and memory which the human being is likely to put upon it—and a billion times more than that quantity, too."—The New York "Times Magazine."

thians 15:21, 22) Paul here refers to the Bible account of Adam and Eve, which account Jesus Christ confirmed as accurate. (Mark 10:6-8) The Creator had put the first couple in a garden home, with the happy prospect of endless life in harmony with his will. They had ample healthful food from the various trees and other vegetation. Furthermore, Adam and Eve were perfect humans. Their minds and bodies were without defect, and there was no reason for these to deteriorate, as happens with humans now.—Deuteronomy 32:4; Genesis 1:31.

⁴ Only one restriction was placed on that first human pair. God said: "As for the tree of the knowledge of good and bad you must not eat from it, for in the day you eat from it you will positively die." (Genesis 2:17) By complying with this limitation, they would show recognition of God's authority to determine what is good and what is bad for humans. In time, they set their own standards of good and bad. (Genesis 3:6, 7) By disobeying God's plainly stated command, they committed what the Bible calls "sin." In both Hebrew and Greek, "to sin" means "to miss [the mark]." Adam and Eve missed the mark or fell short of perfect obedience. They no longer reflected Jehovah's perfection, and they brought upon themselves God's just sentence.—Luke 16:10.

⁵ Adam and Eve's sin affected both them and us. Why us? Well, God did not execute them immediately. Showing consideration for all that was involved, Jehovah let the first pair bring forth children. But Adam and Eve were no longer perfect; when they sinned they began to deteriorate physically and mentally. So they could not produce perfect children. (Job 14:4) The situation

could be likened to that of a couple today who have a genetic defect that they pass on to their children. We inherited the defect of sin, for we all stem from an imperfect first pair. Paul explains: "Through one man [Adam] sin entered into the world and death through sin, and thus death spread to all men because they had all sinned."—Romans 5:12; Psalm 51:5.

[6] Was the situation hopeless? Both history and the Bible confirm that left up to humans it would have been. We are unable to cleanse ourselves of the stain of sin or to release ourselves from God's condemnation. If there was to be a release, God would provide it. His law was broken, so he would be the One to determine how perfect justice could be met and a release provided. Jehovah God showed his undeserved kindness by making provision for relief to Adam and Eve's offspring, including us. The Bible explains what the provision is and how we may benefit.

[7] These passages offer the basis for understanding the matter:

"God loved the world [of mankind] so much that he gave his only-begotten Son, in order that everyone exercising faith in him might not be destroyed but have everlasting life."—John 3:16.

"The Son of man [Jesus] came, not to be ministered to, but to minister and to give his soul a ransom in exchange for many."—Mark 10:45.

"All have sinned and fall short of the glory of God, and it is as a free gift that they are being declared righteous by his undeserved kindness through the release by the ransom paid by Christ

Why is the solution to sickness and death up to God?
(6, 7)

Jesus. God set him forth as an offering [that covers] through faith in his blood."—Romans 3:23-25.

WHAT IS "THE RANSOM"?

8 Two of those texts mention a "ransom." That, basically, is a price paid to set a captive free. (Isaiah 43:3) We often hear the word used with reference to money for releasing a kidnap victim. In our case, the captive is mankind. Adam sold us into bondage to sin, with resulting sickness and death. (Romans 7:14) What valuable thing could redeem mankind and open up for us the prospect of life free from the effects of sin?

9 Recall that the Bible says that Jesus 'gave his *life* as a ransom.' (Mark 10:45) We can see from this that a human life was needed. By sinning, Adam had forfeited perfect human life. To open the way for mankind to regain life in perfection another perfect human life was needed to balance or buy back what Adam had lost. This emphasizes why no imperfect descendant of Adam could provide the ransom. As Psalm 49:7, 8 says: "Man could never redeem himself or pay his ransom to God: it costs so much to redeem his life, it is beyond him."—*Jerusalem Bible.*

10 To provide the ransom price, God sent his perfect spirit Son from heaven to be born as a human. An angel explained to the chaste virgin Mary how God would make sure that Jesus would be perfect at birth: "Power of the Most High will overshadow you. For that reason also what is born will be called holy, God's Son." (Luke 1:35; Galatians 4:4) Jesus, not having an imperfect

---

How has a ransom been provided? (8-11)

human father, was free of inherited sin.—1 Peter 2:22; Hebrews 7:26.

¹¹ After living as a human in full accord with God's will, Christ gave up his perfect human life. It was a life such as Adam had when created, so Jesus became a "corresponding ransom for all." (1 Timothy 2:5, 6; 1 Corinthians 15:45) Yes, it was "for all" in that he paid the price to purchase the entire human family. Accordingly, the Bible says that we have been "bought with a price." (1 Corinthians 6:20) God, through Jesus' death, thus laid the basis for counteracting what Adam did in bringing sin, sickness and death on mankind. This truth can have real meaning in making our lives happy.

HOW CAN OUR SINS BE FORGIVEN?

¹² It is fine to know from the Bible that Jesus paid the ransom price. But there still is something that can be a barrier to our having God's approval and blessing. That is the fact that we personally are sinners. We 'miss the mark' many times. Paul wrote: "All have sinned and fall short of the glory of God." (Romans 3:23) What can be done about that? How can we become acceptable to our righteous God, Jehovah?

¹³ Certainly we would not expect God to look with approval on us if we continued in a course that we knew to be contrary to his will. We must repent sincerely of our wrong desires, speech and conduct, and then endeavor to conform to his standards set out in the Bible. (Acts 17:30) Still our sins—past and present—need to be covered over. Jesus' ransom sacrifice serves us here. Paul gives an indication of this, writing that God 'set

What basis is there for our sins to be forgiven? (12-17)

forth Jesus as an *offering that covers through* *faith in his blood.*'—Romans 3:24, 25.

[14] The apostle was here referring to something that God arranged long before and that was to picture or to point forward to Christ. In ancient Israel animal sacrifices for sins were regularly offered on behalf of the people. And individuals

The sacrifices in Israel pointed forward to Jesus' ransom sacrifice

themselves could make guilt offerings for special cases of wrongdoing. (Leviticus 16:1-34; 5:1-6, 17-19) God accepted these blood sacrifices as atoning for or canceling out human sins. But this did not bring lasting relief, for the Bible says that "it is not possible for the blood of bulls and of goats to take sins away." (Hebrews 10:3, 4) However, these features of worship involving priests, temples, altars and offerings were "an illustration" or "a shadow of the good things to come" involving Jesus' sacrifice.—Hebrews 9:6-9, 11, 12; 10:1.

[15] The Bible shows how important this is to our obtaining forgiveness, saying: "By means of him we have the release by *ransom* through the *blood* of that one [Jesus], yes, the *forgiveness* of our trespasses." (Ephesians 1:7; 1 Peter 2:24) So, in addition to his death's providing the ransom, it can cover our sins; we can have our sins forgiven. But something is required of us. Since we have been purchased, yes, "bought with a price" by Christ's ransom, we must be willing to accept Jesus as our Lord or Owner and obey him. (1 Corinthians 6:11, 20; Hebrews 5:9) Consequently, we need to repent of our sins and to couple this with faith in the sacrifice of Jesus our Lord.

[16] If we do so, we do not have to wait for forgiveness until God relieves mankind of all the effects of sin, putting an end to sickness and death. The Scriptures speak of this forgiveness as something that we can enjoy right now, resulting in a clean conscience before God.—1 John 2:12.

[17] Jesus' sacrifice should, therefore, have very personal meaning for us each day. By means of it God can forgive the wrongs we commit. The apostle John explains: "I am writing you these

things that you may not commit a sin. And yet, if anyone does commit a sin, we have a helper with the Father, Jesus Christ, a righteous one." (1 John 2:1; Luke 11:2-4) This is a primary Bible teaching and is vital to our lasting happiness. —1 Corinthians 15:3.

WHAT WILL YOU DO?

[18] How do you react to what the Bible says about the cause of sickness and death, the ransom and the provision for forgiveness through Jesus Christ? A person might take in these details mentally without its touching his heart and life. But more is required of us.

[19] Do we appreciate God's love in providing the ransom? The apostle John wrote: "God loved the world *so much* that he gave his only-begotten Son." (John 3:16) Remember that the humans involved were sinners, alienated from God. (Romans 5:10; Colossians 1:21) Would you give up your dearest one in behalf of persons most of whom showed little or no interest in you? Yet Jehovah had his pure and faithful Son, his beloved Firstborn, come to earth to face contempt, shame and death in order to provide relief for humankind. That moved Paul to write: "God recommends his own love to us in that, while we were yet sinners, Christ died for us."—Romans 5:8.

[20] The Son showed his love, too. When the time came, he willingly lowered himself to become a man. He slaved for imperfect humans, teaching and healing them. And, though innocent, he accepted ridicule, torture and a shameful death at the hands of enemies of the truth. As an aid to

How do you respond to what God and Jesus have done? (1 John 4:9-11) (18-21)

appreciating this, take the time to read the account of Jesus' betrayal, trial, abuse and execution, as recorded in Luke 22:47 through 23:47.

[21] How will you respond to all of this? Certainly a person should not let his acceptance of the loving provision of the ransom become an excuse for wrong conduct. That would be missing its purpose, and it could even result in sin that is beyond forgiveness. (Hebrews 10:26, 29; Numbers 15:30) Instead, we ought to endeavor to live in a way that will bring honor to our Creator. And faith in the grand provision made through his Son should move us to talk to others about it, helping them to appreciate how they too can benefit. —Acts 4:12; Romans 10:9, 10; James 2:26; 2 Corinthians 5:14, 15.

[22] When Jesus Christ was on earth he said that he could extend God's forgiveness of sins. Some enemies criticized him for that. So Jesus proved it by healing a paralyzed man. (Luke 5:17-26) Hence, just as sin produced physical effects on mankind, the forgiveness of sins can result in benefits. It is important to know that. What Jesus did on earth shows that God can bring an end to sickness and dying. That is in accord with what Jesus Christ himself said, namely, that Jehovah God gave his Son so that persons with faith might have "everlasting life." (John 3:16) But how? When? And what about our loved ones who have already died?

Forgiveness of our sins can involve what prospect? (22)

12

Death Is Not an Unbeatable Enemy

DEATH is an enemy of life. Each funeral shows that death is like a king who seems to conquer all. (Romans 5:14) Some trees live more than 1,000 years; some fish, 150; yet man's years are only 70 or 80 before death swallows him up.—Psalm 90:10.

² With good cause the Bible presents death as an enemy. Though we seem to have a built-in desire to live and learn endlessly, no matter what a man has learned, what his skills are, how highly he is thought of by friends and relatives, death claims him. (Ecclesiastes 3:11; 7:2) Most persons, agreeing that death is an enemy, try desperately to delay its victory. Others frantically seek all the pleasure they can from life before they are defeated.

³ Down through history, though, many people have believed that there is life after death. The Greek philosopher Plato taught that we have an immortal soul that survives the body. Do we? Interest in this has been stimulated by recent stories of persons who supposedly died, were revived and later described what they 'saw beyond death's door.' Are the dead alive somewhere? Can death be conquered?

POINT FOR DISCUSSION: Why should we examine "enemy" death? (Job 14:1, 2) (1-3)

DEATH'S FIRST VICTORY

[4] The Bible shows that humans were created to live, not to die. God placed Adam and Eve in a delightful garden where they could enjoy life. He designated one of the trees "the tree of life." Likely if Adam and Eve had proved their appreciation and loyalty to God, he would have let them eat from that tree, symbolizing his grant of everlasting life for them. (Genesis 1:30; 2:7-9) However, Adam and Eve chose to disobey God. Their sin brought upon them the sentence of death.—Genesis 3:17-19.

[5] For us to understand whether death is indeed an unbeatable enemy, we need to examine the result of death's victory over Adam and Eve. Did they "die" completely? Or was that "death" only a transition to a different kind of life?

[6] After Adam foolishly sinned, Jehovah kept to his just and righteous word. He told Adam:

"In the sweat of your face you will eat bread until you return to the ground, for out of it you were taken. For dust you are and to dust you will return."—Genesis 3:19.

What did that mean for Adam and for us today?

[7] The earlier account of Adam's creation tells us: "God proceeded to form the man out of dust from the ground and to blow into his nostrils the breath of life, and the man came to be a living soul." (Genesis 2:7) Think what that means. Before God created him from the dust, there was no Adam. Hence, after he died and returned to the dust, there would be no Adam.—Genesis 5:3-5.

How did death come upon mankind? (4, 5)
What did "death" mean for Adam? (6, 7)

ARE THE DEAD CONSCIOUS?

[8] Many persons might be surprised at the thought that once Adam died he no longer existed. Yet the stated penalty for sin—Adam's dying and going back to dust—contained no hint of continued life. Death is the opposite of life, whether for a man or a beast. Both have the same "spirit," or life force. Thus the Bible comments:

> "There is an eventuality as respects the sons of mankind and an eventuality as respects the beast, and they have the same eventuality. As the one dies, so the other dies; and they all have but one spirit, so that there is no superiority of the man over the beast . . . They have all come to be from the dust, and they are all returning to the dust."—Ecclesiastes 3:19, 20.

[9] Does that mean that the dead have no thoughts or feelings? Ecclesiastes 9:4, 5 answers: "A live dog is better off than a dead lion. For the living are conscious that they will die; but as for the dead, they are conscious of nothing at all." When a person dies, "his thoughts do perish," he has no ability either to feel or to work.—Psalm 146: 3, 4; 31:17.

[10] Since the Bible assures us that the dead are unconscious and without feel-

How could you show someone from the Bible whether the dead are conscious? (8-11)

DUST

ADAM

DUST

ing, that means that death ends pain and suffering. Job, a faithful servant of God, knew this. When he was suffering a painful disease he said:

"Why from the womb did I not proceed to die? . . . Why was it that knees confronted me, and why breasts that I should take suck? For by now I should have lain down that I might be undisturbed; I should have slept then; I should be at rest."—Job 3:11-13.

¹¹ But is this taking into account the soul?

¹² Simply put, the Scriptures teach that your soul is you. What we have already read in Genesis 2:7 shows that. Recall that God formed man's body from dust. Then God provided life and the breath needed to sustain it. What was the result? According to God's own Word, the man "came to be a living soul [Hebrew, *nephesh*]." (Genesis 2:7) Adam was not *given* a soul, nor did he *come to have* a soul. He *was a soul*. In teaching this, the Bible is consistent throughout. Many centuries later the apostle Paul quoted Genesis 2:7, writing: "The first man Adam became a living soul [Greek, *psykhe*]."—1 Corinthians 15:45.

¹³ The Hebrew word *nephesh* and the Greek word *psykhe,* found in these texts, are translated in various ways. At Ezekiel 18:4 and Matthew 10:28 you will find that, in many Bible versions, they are rendered as "soul." Elsewhere those same original words are translated as "being," "creature," or "person." These are valid translations of the original words, and a comparison of them shows that the soul is the creature or person himself, not some invisible part of man. The Bible applies the same original-language words to animals, showing that they are souls or have life as souls. —Genesis 2:19; Leviticus 11:46; Revelation 8:9.

According to the Bible, what is a "soul"? (12, 13)

[14] As a soul, Adam, or any of us, could eat, get hungry and grow tired. In the original Hebrew, the Bible says that souls do all these things. (Deuteronomy 23:24; Proverbs 19:15; 25:25) In stating a prohibition that applied to the Israelites regarding work on a certain day, God made clear another important point about the soul, saying: "As for any soul that will do any sort of work on this very day, I must destroy that soul from among his people." (Leviticus 23:30) Hence, the Bible, here and in many other texts, shows that a soul can die.—Ezekiel 18:4, 20; Psalm 33:19.

[15] Knowing such Bible truths can help us to evaluate recent stories about persons who supposedly died (there being no detectable heartbeat or brain activity), but who were revived and thereafter told about having floated outside their body. One possibility is that they may have had hallucinations caused by medication or the brain's oxygen-starved condition. Whether that is the full explanation or not, we know with certainty that no invisible soul left the body.

[16] Also, if the dead are totally unconscious and no "soul" floats off from the body, then there can be no fiery hell awaiting the souls of the wicked, can there? Yet many churches teach that the wicked will be tormented after they die. On learning the truth about the dead, some persons have been justifiably disturbed, asking: 'Why did not our religion tell us the truth about the dead?' What is your own reaction?—Compare Jeremiah 7:31.

Can a soul die, and what implications does this have? (14-16)

'It is noteworthy that in the New Testament we do not find hellfire to be a part of the primitive preaching. There are some indications in the New Testament that the ultimate fate of those who refuse God's offer of salvation may be annihilation rather than eternal punishment.'—"A Dictionary of Christian Theology," edited by Alan Richardson.

WHAT FUTURE FOR THE DEAD?

[17] If the only future for persons now living were unconsciousness in death, then death would be an unbeatable enemy. But the Bible shows that it is not.

[18] The immediate future for a person after death is in the grave. The languages in which the Bible was written had words for the place of the dead, mankind's common grave. In Hebrew it was termed *Sheol*. It was called *Hades* in Greek. These words have been translated in some Bibles by terms such as "grave," "pit" or "hell." Regardless of how they are rendered, the meaning of the original-language terms is not a hot place of suffering but is the grave of the unconscious dead. We read:

"All that your hand finds to do, do with your very power, for there is no work nor devising nor knowledge nor wisdom in Sheol [hell, Douay Version; the grave, Authorized Version], the place to which you are going."—Ecclesiastes 9:10.

The apostle Peter assures us that upon death even Jesus went to the grave, to *Sheol, Hades* or hell. —Acts 2:31; compare Psalm 16:10.

What happens to a person after death? (17-20)

¹⁹ Of course, a dead person has no power to change his condition. (Job 14:12) So is unconsciousness in death all the future there is? For some, yes. The Bible teaches that persons who are totally rejected by God will remain dead forever. —2 Thessalonians 1:6-9.

²⁰ The ancient Jews believed that persons who were extremely wicked would have no future beyond death. The Jews did not bury such ones. Rather, they tossed the corpses into a valley outside Jerusalem where fires were kept burning to dispose of garbage. This was the Valley of Hinnom, or Gehenna. Drawing upon this practice, Jesus used Gehenna as a symbol of complete destruction, with no future prospects. (Matthew 5: 29, 30) For example, he said:

"Do not become fearful of those who kill the body but cannot kill the soul [or, prospects to live as a soul]; but rather be in fear of him [God] that can destroy both soul and body in Gehenna."—Matthew 10:28.

Jesus' words, however, give us reason for hope that many who have died will live again in the future, thus overcoming death.

VICTORY THROUGH RESURRECTION

²¹ God, in one of history's most important acts, raised Jesus Christ to life after he had been dead for days. Jesus became a living spirit creature, as he had been before coming to earth. (1 Corinthians 15:42-45; 1 Peter 3:18) Hundreds of persons saw Jesus appear after he was resurrected. (Acts 2:22-24; 1 Corinthians 15:3-8) These witnesses were willing to risk their lives in support of their faith in Jesus' resurrection. The resur-

---

How is victory over death possible? (21, 22)

rection of Jesus proves that death is not an un-beatable enemy. Victory over death is possible! —1 Corinthians 15:54-57.

²² Further victories over death are also possible. Persons can come back to human life on earth. Jehovah, who cannot lie, assures us in his Word "that there is going to be a resurrection of both the righteous [persons who knew of and did God's will] and the unrighteous [ones who did not practice righteousness]."—Acts 24:15.

²³ We can have confidence in God's ability to bring persons back to human life. Men are able

Why can the future be thrilling? (23-25)

Lazarus' resurrection shows that death can be overcome

to record on film or videotape the image, voice
and mannerisms of a person. Cannot God do much
more? His memory is far more expansive than
any film or tape, so he can perfectly re-create
those he wants to resurrect. (Psalm 147:4) He has
already demonstrated this. The Bible contains a
number of accounts of God's using his Son to
bring humans back to life. You can read two of
these exciting accounts at John 11:5-44 and Luke
7:11-17. With good reason men who worshiped
God in the past looked forward to the time when
he would remember and resurrect them. It would
be like waking them from unconscious sleep.—Job
14:13-15.

²⁴ Those past resurrections must have overjoyed
relatives and friends. But those resurrections defeated death only temporarily, for the resurrected
ones eventually died again. Nonetheless, they offer
us an exciting preview, because the Bible points
to a coming "better resurrection." (Hebrews 11:
35) It will be much, much better because those
coming back to life on earth will not have to
die again. That will mean a far greater victory
over death.—John 11:25, 26.

²⁵ What the Bible says about how God can and
will defeat death certainly indicates his loving
interest in humans. It should help us to understand Jehovah's personality and draw us closer to
him. These truths also help us to have balance,
for we are safeguarded against the morbid fear
of death that preys on many. We can have the
happy hope of even seeing our deceased relatives
and loved ones again when, through the resurrection, death is defeated.—1 Thessalonians 4:13;
Luke 23:43.

13

Communicating with the Spirit Realm

THE compulsion to communicate runs deep."
With that statement, the book *Machines*
began a chapter on the radio. By radio we can
communicate with persons around the globe or
even hear from astronauts in outer space.

2 Radio communication is now an accepted part
of life. But many persons ignore or misunderstand
a more important type of communication—with
the spirit realm.

SPEAKING TO THE CREATOR

3 Centuries before radio was invented, King
David wrote:

"To my sayings do give ear, O Jehovah ... Do pay
attention to the sound of my cry for help, O my King
and my God, because to you I pray."—Psalm 5:1, 2.

Does it not seem reasonable that the highest intelligence in the universe can "give ear" to what
we say in prayer if he desires to do so? And is it
not sensible for us to seek help from God, who
can give us the very best guidance?—Psalm 65:2.

4 A transmitter and a receiver are necessary in
radio communication. But what do we need in

POINT FOR DISCUSSION: Why should we be interested in
communicating with the Creator? (1-3)
What is needed for acceptable prayers? (1 Peter 3:12)
(4, 5)

order to contact Jehovah in prayer? The first requirement is faith. "He that approaches God must believe that he is and that he becomes the rewarder of those earnestly seeking him." (Hebrews 11:6) Also, a person must be attuned to God's moral standards and ways. Otherwise God will no more listen to him than an upright person would listen to a radio program that he viewed as morally repugnant.—1 John 3:22; Isaiah 1:15

⁵ Jehovah does not have a rigid format for acceptable prayers. Whether you pray out loud or silently, he can "hear." You can pray when standing, seated, kneeling or lying in bed. (1 Samuel 1:12, 13; 1 Kings 8:54) No special words or religious language are needed. More important are sincerity and a humble spirit. Note how Jesus illustrated this at Luke 18:10-14.

⁶ Individually, we can approach Jehovah in prayer at any time. However, he also welcomes united prayers, such as from a congregation of Christians. By their listening to the prayers at the congregation meetings some who never prayed before have learned how to employ this vital communication. Family groups, too, can and should pray together. One opportunity is at meal times, following Jesus' example in thanking God for the food that he made available.—Mark 8:6

⁷ You may know of persons who have prayed but who complain that they get no answer. Why? Christ told his followers: "If you ask the Father for anything he will give it to you in my name." Jesus Christ, and no other person, is the way of approach to God. Might the problem be a failure to appreciate this? (John 16:23; 14:6) Also, what

What can we learn from the Bible about the nature of our prayers? (6-8)

lid Jesus mean by "anything"? The apostle John hows that it is "anything" that is 'in accord with 'ehovah's will.' We would hardly expect a righeous God to accept prayers for wrong, immoral r greedy ends. (1 John 5:14) Yet many pray or instant wealth or power over others. It is no vonder, then, that God does not respond to such rayers. Requests for our valid personal needs hould come after matters such as God's will eing done on earth.—Matthew 6:9-11.

Daily we can communicate with God through prayer

⁸ Prayer affords opportunities for us to tal
to God as to a loving father, to express our joy
our troubles and needs. If you have not been doin
that regularly, do not put it off. Your having
trusting relationship with God and being able t
communicate with him at any time will give yo
much peace of mind and bring happiness. Yo
can unburden yourself, being sure of his interes
in you.—Psalm 86:1-6; Philippians 4:6, 7.

RESPONSE FROM THE SPIRIT REALM

⁹ One of the main subjects of prayer should b
our need for wisdom and guidance from Go
(Psalm 27:11; 119:34-36; James 1:5) In wha
manner will God respond? In ancient times, h
occasionally gave verbal messages, speakin
through angels or human prophets. But the apos
tle Paul says that God has now "spoken to us b
means of a Son," whose teachings and life patter
are set out in the Bible. (Hebrews 1:1, 2; 2:1-3
John 20:31) So, rather than expecting God t
speak to us personally, we should seek hel
through the means he has chosen to use, th
Bible. With this in mind, we should follow u
prayers for guidance by diligently studying hi
Word. (Proverbs 2:1-5) Added help is availabl
through devoted Christians who regularly mee
to study and discuss the Bible.—2 Timothy 2:1, 2

¹⁰ In answer to our prayers, God can also aid u
personally through his spirit. With this, he help
Christians to understand his Word and apply i
(John 16:7-13) David prayed: "Teach me to d
your will . . . Your spirit is good; may it lead m
in the land of uprightness."—Psalm 143:10.

How can we receive communication from God? (9, 10

ARE THERE EVIL PERSONS IN THE SPIRIT REALM?

¹¹ Not only does the Bible assure us that Jehovah, his Son and angels exist in the spirit realm, and that we may communicate with God by prayer. Just as reliably the Scriptures show that there are intelligent spirit persons who are now very wicked, specifically Satan and his demons.

¹² Some persons feel that "the Devil" is just a carry-over from an old superstition or myth. Others think that when the Bible mentions "Satan" it is referring simply to a principle of evil.

¹³ However, Matthew 4:1-11 tells us of a time when Satan offered three very specific temptations to Jesus. Certainly, the Satan here referred to was no evil principle within Jesus, for the Son of God is free of evil and sin. (Hebrews 7:26; 4:8, 9) No, Satan is a real person. This is also borne out by the account at Job 1:6-12, which tells of Satan's appearing before Jehovah.

¹⁴ But what of Satan's origin? We know that Jehovah is the Creator of all things and that "perfect is his activity." (Deuteronomy 32:4; Revelation 4:11) Hence, is it not logical that Satan must at one time have been an upright spirit person created by Jehovah along with other angels? How, then, did he become corrupt? James 1:14, 15 gives us a clue:

"Each one is tried by being drawn out and enticed by his own desire. Then the desire, when it has become fertile, gives birth to sin."

¹⁵ From what has occurred among men, we know that even someone in a trusted position

---

How can we know that Satan exists? And what is his origin? (11-15)

might see how he could misuse a situation in order to get more power. It appears that this is what occurred with one of God's angels. Being a free moral agent, this spirit creature chose a bad course, perhaps believing that he could become like God, with humans following him. What happened is evidently comparable to the experience of a king of Tyre, as related at Ezekiel 28: 1-19. This man had been in a favored position relative to ancient Israel, but he became puffed up with pride, leading to his downfall. Similarly pride led to the ruin of the one who made himself Satan, a resister of God.

[16] An understanding of Satan's existence sheds light on the events in the garden of Eden that resulted in our being imperfect, sinners, subject to sickness and death. With his above-human intelligence, Satan used a serpent to communicate a lying, fatal proposition to Eve. (Genesis 3:1-5) Accordingly, Revelation 12:9 calls Satan "the original serpent." And Jesus said this one did not "stand fast in the truth," but became "the father of the lie" and a "manslayer."—John 8:44.

[17] Satan is not the only spirit creature who rebelled. The history in Genesis 6:1-3 explains that in Noah's day some angels—perhaps stimulated by Satan's rebellion—took on human bodies so as to have sexual pleasure with women. This was unnatural and corrupt. (Jude 6, 7) When God wiped out the wickedness on earth by a global flood, these disobedient angels returned to the spirit realm, but now on Satan's side, as demons. (2 Peter 2:4, 5) The well-known Greek and Roman mythologies about gods that moved back and forth

---

How does our knowing of Satan and the demons aid us? (16, 17)

etween heaven and earth may be distortions of he facts about the disobedient angels as reported n the Bible.

WICKED INFLUENCE FROM THE SPIRIT REALM

[18] The wicked spirits are not interested in our welfare but are bent on deceiving and misleading humans, turning them away from God. The apostle Paul called Satan "the god of this system of things" who "has blinded the minds of the unbelievers" so that they might not learn the "good news" about Christ. (2 Corinthians 4:4) He has been quite successful in this.

[19] One tactic that he has used is by encouraging the view that there is no Devil or Satan. He is like a criminal who spreads the idea that a crime syndicate does not exist, thus lulling persons into a false security. Another tactic is reflected in the horrible deeds committed by religious zealots—crusades, inquisitions, the blessing of warfare. These have caused many sensitive persons to turn away from Jehovah God, mistakenly thinking that the churches represent him.

[20] Recall, too, that the apostle Paul said that Satan is "the god of this system of things." Some persons scoff at the idea that Satan is maneuvering the nations. But when Satan offered Christ authority over the nations, Jesus did not deny that the Devil has power over the political kingdoms. (Luke 4:5-8) And does it not seem that there is some evil force behind world affairs today? With this in mind, read what Revelation 12:9, 12 says about Satan's efforts.

In what way have wicked spirits affected humans? 2 Corinthians 11:13-15) (18-20)

AVOIDING CONTACT WITH WICKED SPIRITS

[21] Scientists have done research on what i
known as ESP (extrasensory perception). This in
cludes phenomena such as a person's knowing
others' thoughts, describing events or objects tha
he could never have seen or learned of, and using
'mind over matter' to influence such things as th
fall of dice. The psychic researchers have tried t
exclude the possibility of trickery, yet they can
not explain these superhuman feats. Might wha
the Scriptures say be the explanation?

[22] Satan and the demons can directly affec
humans and their affairs. For example, a girl i
ancient Philippi, in Greece, was able to make pre
dictions. How? The historical record says that "a
spirit, a demon of divination," influenced the girl'
utterances. The apostle Paul helped her to ge
free from the demon.—Acts 16:16-18.

[23] Because the demons are real and powerful
God's Word repeatedly warns against involvemen
with them. It condemns the use of spells (as in
black magic or voodoo), the consulting of me
diums or a person's trying to contact the dead
(Deuteronomy 18:10-12; Leviticus 20:6, 27; Ga
latians 5:19-21) Those warnings are still timely
You may have observed the widespread interes
in psychic phenomena and the occult. Many film
and novels have featured 'the spirits' or man'
efforts to exorcise, or cast out, demons. The us
of Ouija boards or astrology for guidance i
common.

[24] Communication with wicked spirits is dan

What practices can involve a person with wicke
spirits? (21-23)
How can you protect yourself from harmful commu
nication with the spirit realm? (24-28)

gerous. Reports indicate that once the demons gain influence over a person, they can do much harm—physically, mentally and emotionally. (Compare Matthew 8:28-33.) They have harassed persons, making noises at night, causing objects to move about, fondling sex organs and causing illness. Their "voices" have even driven persons to insanity, murder or suicide.

²⁵ Of course, some "strange" occurrences may result from physical problems, such as disturbances of body chemistry, which may affect the mind and the senses. But it would be foolish simply to dismiss the existence of Satan and the demons. Do not underestimate the seriousness of the Bible's warning about them.

²⁶ If a person is being harassed by the demons, is there any way to get relief? God is not now using humans to heal the sick, cast out demons or raise the dead, as he used the apostles. But he

will help someone break free from "the authority of Satan." (Acts 26:18; Ephesians 6:12) It is necessary to turn to Jehovah in prayer, using his name and earnestly seeking his help. (Proverbs 18:10) Also, one must resist demonic suggestions, as did Jesus, ceasing spiritistic practices and needless fellowship with those pursuing demonism. —Matthew 4:1-11; 2 Corinthians 6:14-17.

[27] Additionally, reports show that the demons often keep in contact with a human through an object, so it is important to get rid of items formerly used in spiritism (charms, crystal balls, and so forth). The Bible tells us that some who had practiced magical arts in ancient Ephesus did that.—Acts 19:18-20.

[28] Yet there is no need to be in constant dread of wicked spirits. Rather, the Bible urges us to clothe ourselves with spiritual armor:

"Stand firm, therefore, with your loins girded about with TRUTH, and having on the breastplate of RIGHTEOUSNESS, and with your feet shod with the equipment of the GOOD NEWS OF PEACE. Above all things, take up the large shield of FAITH, with which you will be able to quench all the wicked one's burning missiles. Also, accept the helmet of SALVATION, and the sword of the spirit, that is, GOD'S WORD, while . . . you carry on PRAYER on every occasion."—Ephesians 6:14-18.

As God's Word here shows, an excellent safeguard against unwanted communication with wicked spirits is regular communication with Jehovah through prayer. The Bible fittingly says: "Subject yourselves, therefore, to God; but oppose the Devil, and he will flee from you."—James 4:7.

14

Wickedness—
Why Does God Permit It?

I F A friend of yours were robbed, raped or murdered and the criminal let go free, would you not feel frustration, hurt and anger? Such crimes and injustices are just a small reflection of what has befallen mankind.

² History is a long record of brutal wars, crushing poverty, crime and oppression. As a result, some persons have come to doubt the very existence of God. We know that there is convincing evidence that the Creator exists. (Hebrews 3:4; Romans 1:20) But there is wickedness too. For this reason, even many who believe in God wonder, 'Does he really care about us?' They ask, 'If God does care, why has he permitted wickedness for so long?'

³ Philosophers and clergymen have often dealt

POINT FOR DISCUSSION: Why is it reasonable to examine what the Bible says about wickedness? (1-3)

Dr. W. R. Inge, who was dean of St. Paul's Cathedral, London, some years ago said:

"All my life I have struggled to find the purpose of living. I have tried to answer three problems which always seemed to me to be fundamental: the problem of eternity; the problem of human personality; and the problem of evil. I have failed. I have solved none of them."

with this matter, but have no satisfying answers.
What does God himself say?

GOD ANSWERS: 'I DO CARE'

⁴ Based on our experience, we can appreciate
the Hebrew prophet Habakkuk's reaction to violence and injustice. He lived at a time when the
Jews had fallen into many bad practices, which
sorely troubled Habakkuk and moved him to ask
God:

*"Why do you make me look at injustice? Why
do you tolerate wrong? Destruction and violence
are before me; there is strife, and conflict abounds.
Therefore the law is paralyzed, and justice never
prevails. The wicked hem in the righteous, so that
justice is perverted."—Habakkuk 1:3, 4,* New International Version.

Though convinced of Jehovah's righteousness,
Habakkuk was distressed by the violence and injustice among his people. Also, at that time the
Babylonians were on the rampage, terrorizing and
despoiling other nations. It seemed that wickedness prevailed everywhere. The prophet Habakkuk
wondered why God, who could see it, seemed to
do nothing.—Habakkuk 1:13.

⁵ In a vision Jehovah assured Habakkuk that
the seeming prosperity of the wicked was only
temporary. God not only saw what was occurring,
but also cared. He had an "appointed time" for
meting out divine justice. Even if humans thought
that this was delaying, Habakkuk was assured,
"It will without fail come true. It will not be late."
—Habakkuk 2:3.

What can we learn from Habakkuk on this matter?
(4-8)

⁶ Further showing God's care, he alerted Habakkuk to a challenge facing humans in the meantime. Jehovah said: "But as for the righteous one, by his faithfulness he will keep living." (Habakkuk 2:4) Would Habakkuk meet the challenge, doing what was right and moral despite what those around him did? He needed to display faith that God would handle matters properly in his "appointed time."

⁷ History tells us what happened. When the time arrived, God acted to end violence and injustice on the part of the Jews. The land was conquered and many of the people were taken captive. Later, God had an accounting with Babylon. As Jehovah foretold through his prophets, the Medes and the Persians under Cyrus defeated the seemingly all-powerful Babylonian Empire. —Jeremiah 51:11, 12; Isaiah 45:1; Daniel 5:22-31.

⁸ This small-scale illustration shows that our Creator does not close his eyes to wickedness. He is aware of it and he does care. (Compare Genesis 18:20, 21; 19:13.) That being so, why has God allowed wickedness to continue until now? To understand the Bible's logical explanation, we need to go back to when human troubles began.

UNIVERSAL ISSUES ARISE

⁹ As recounted in Genesis chapter three, the Devil questioned Eve about her obeying God's command not to eat from a specially designated tree. Eve answered that disobedience would bring the sentence of death. But Satan replied:

"You positively will not die. For God knows that

How did universally vital issues arise in Eden? What were they? (9-12)

in the very day of your eating from it your eyes are bound to be opened and you are bound to be like God, knowing good and bad."—Genesis 3:1-5.

Satan here brought up challenges or issues that involved all of God's creatures, men and angels.

¹⁰ For one thing the Devil *challenged God's honesty.* Reflect on the implications of this. *If* God were not truthful in this matter, could he be trusted in anything else? Would his creatures on earth or in heaven always have to be suspicious about what God said? We know today how suspicious persons are of politicians who govern through the use of lies.—Compare Psalm 5:9.

¹¹ Satan's claim that God is deceitful and withholds things that are good for his creatures also raised the issue, *Does God deserve to rule?* The question of the rightfulness of God's way of ruling involved all the universe.

¹² Additionally, Satan was contending that humans can get along without God, that they can and should rule themselves. The question was put before men and angels, *Can humans successfully govern their affairs independent of God?*

¹³ Those serious moral issues demanded complete settlement. The way in which God chose to do that clearly shows his wisdom and his interest in our welfare, both now and in the future. God allowed time to pass, during which all intelligent creatures could see the evidence. To appreciate this, consider how you would act if someone publicly claimed that you were not a good family member, that you lied and exercised authority through instilling fear. An insecure person might loudly protest or even fight the accuser. But

In what way were the issues to be settled? (13-15)

secure in the knowledge that the charge was false, you could dispel questions simply by allowing time for all to observe your ways and the fine results in your family.—Matthew 12:33.

[14] What evidence has time revealed on the issues raised in Eden? As God forewarned, human disobedience has resulted in death, preceded by sickness and old age. So God was not dishonest in his warning, and there was no basis in this for challenging the rightfulness of his rulership. There is also proof that man cannot set his own standards, ruling himself independently of God. No form of human government has been able to prevent wars, corruption, oppression, crime and injustice. This confirms what the Bible says: "To earthling man his way does not belong. It does not belong to man who is walking even to direct his steps." (Jeremiah 10:23) Further, time has proved that men cannot end suffering; rather, that they often cause it.

[15] The suffering is felt by sincere persons who are willing to accept God's rulership and standards. With them in mind, God is going to act against those carrying on wickedness, even as he did on the small scale mentioned in the book of Habakkuk. Jehovah will eliminate all in heaven and on earth who are responsible for wickedness and suffering. Just as God told Habakkuk, there is an "appointed time" for this. We can be sure that "it will without fail come true. It will not be late."—Habakkuk 2:3.

BENEFITING FROM THE TIME ALLOWED

[16] As to God's permitting evil, many persons think only about man's suffering. They fail to

How are we involved in another issue that needs settlement? (16-20)

appreciate the important issues that are being
settled. Also, they may overlook the benefits that
they can receive because God has allowed time
for the settlement.—2 Peter 3:9.

¹⁷ The time God has allowed for settling these
matters has been sufficiently long for us to be
born. Whatever pleasures we have enjoyed, it is
because of God's time allowance. Further, we have
been given the opportunity to prove our love for
and loyalty to God. As a challenge, Satan argued
that no human would prove faithful to God, not
even one of whom God could say, "There is no
one like him in the earth, a man blameless and
upright, fearing God and turning aside from bad."
We see this from the Bible book of Job, chapters
1 and 2. Concerning the upright man Job, the
Devil said: "Is it for nothing that Job has feared
God?" Satan claimed that Job did it for selfish
reasons, because God gave him prosperity, but
that if Job were to lose that he would curse God.
(Job 1:7-12) Could Satan turn all men away from
God?

¹⁸ God let Satan bring many troubles on Job.
Job lost his wealth. His children were killed. He
was struck with a loathsome disease. Though not
knowing that Satan was making him the object
of special attack, Job remained faithful to God.
(Job 27:5) He was sure that Jehovah would not
forget him and that the Creator would even resurrect him if he died. (Job 14:13-15) Jehovah never
abandons his loyal ones. In time he stepped in
and undid the damage that Satan had caused.
Job's health was restored. He came to have 10
more beautiful children, together with great
prosperity and a long life. You may read the encouraging details in Job 42:10-17.

¹⁹ This account also helps us to see why God has permitted wickedness. In this way it was proved that some humans would love God despite life's problems and be loyal to him under any test. We do well to ask ourselves, 'Is that how we have reacted despite suffering? Is it how we want to be, thus helping to answer the challenge Satan raised?' (Proverbs 27:11) The book of Job also gives us reason to be confident that God can undo any suffering that humans face while wickedness is being permitted.—Compare 2 Corinthians 4: 16, 17.

²⁰ As God observed and approved of Job and Habakkuk, He is now taking note of hu-

Suffering did not turn Job against God; he endured and was blessed

mans who are loyal to him in the face of evil conditions, and he will not fail to reward them —Malachi 3:16-18.

DO YOU WANT TO LIVE
WHEN WICKEDNESS IS GONE?

[21] The Bible assures us that God purposes to restore the earth to a paradise condition, such as Adam and Eve enjoyed before being disloyal (Luke 23:43; Revelation 21:4, 5) Then there will be complete fulfillment of Bible promises such as:

"The wicked will disappear; you may look for them, but you won't find them; but the humble [or, meek] will possess the land and enjoy prosperity and peace."—Psalm 37:10, 11, Good News Bible; *Proverbs 24:1, 20.*

[22] Many persons complain about evil and suffering, even blaming God for these. But do they truly want the elimination of wickedness, or just of its penalties? Much of his suffering man brings upon himself; he reaps what he sows. (Galatians 6:7; Proverbs 19:3) Immorality produces venereal disease, abortions, divorces. Smoking leads to lung cancer. Drunkenness and drug abuse damage the liver and the brain. Breaking traffic laws causes fatal accidents. Do those who say, 'Why does God permit wickedness? When will he stop it?' really want God to do so? If he did so right now, by preventing these practices, many would complain that he was restricting them.

[23] Hence, God's allowing wickedness lets us show where we stand, what is in our hearts. God told Habakkuk: "As for the righteous one, by his

---

What prospect does the Bible hold out? Meaning what for us? (21-23)

faithfulness he will keep living." That requires cultivating a hatred for what God shows to be bad or evil. (Habakkuk 2:4; Psalm 97:10) Living that way may make us unpopular with some neighbors and associates. (1 Peter 4:3-5) Job and Habakkuk were willing to be different so as to be loyal to God and have his approval. And millions of Jehovah's Witnesses today are likewise proving that it can be done and are enjoying richer, more contented lives.

24 Persons who are following this course are adding to the evidence that Satan is a gross liar. They are proving that humans *can* be faithful to God, confident of the rightfulness and righteousness of his way of rule. God, in turn, knows that such persons can be entrusted with caring for the paradise to be restored on earth. Life then will be so delightful that the sorrows and evils of the past will not come to mind. They will be forgotten just as we have forgotten the pain and sorrow we felt years ago when, as children, we may have scraped a knee.—Isaiah 65:17; John 16:21.

25 That is a delightful prospect and it helps us to see that God's permission of wickedness is just a brief interlude in the outworking of his eternal purpose. The legal, moral issues giving rise to it will be settled for all time.

26 But even understanding why God has permitted wickedness, we rightly want to know: When will it end? When is the "appointed time" for God to end wickedness earth wide? Let us now see.

How can we lastingly benefit from God's having permitted wickedness? (24-26)

15

Is "the End of the World" Near?

"**A**RE You Ready for the End of the World?" asked the Toronto *Star*. That question would make some persons think of reports such as this one:

"Sydney, Australia—Out in the Australian bush, a group of 100 city dwellers who have fled their homes and forsaken the luxuries of present-day life are preparing for what they believe to be the imminent 'end of the world.'"

[2] Yet many persons today worry that "the end" could well result from nuclear war, pollution or other real dangers. For example:

"Science writer Isaac Asimov has counted some 20 ways in which life could become extinct on earth, ranging from the sun dying to famine."—Toronto *Star*.

POINT FOR DISCUSSION: Why should we be interested in "the end of the world"? (1-3)

"Predictions concerning the end of the world have been made since ancient times. . . . Today, however, there are ominous portents that will not go away; 'people problems' that seem insoluble even by the most astute politicians; a lunatic fringe in a nuclear world and mankind's termite-like destruction of his irreplaceable environment."—"The Spectator," Ontario, Canada.

[3] We have, though, a more serious reason for concern based on the reliable Word of God. Many have read in the Bible about "the end of the world." (Matthew 13:39, 40; 24:3, *Authorized Version, New American Bible*) Knowing that whatever God promises will occur, we should want to see what the Bible says about this and how it can affect our lives now and in the future.

AN END—OF WHAT, AND WHEN?

[4] The Scriptures assure us that God will annihilate those who promote evil and suffering. (Psalm 37:28; 145:20) Both Jesus Christ and the apostle Peter compared this coming execution of judgment to the *selective* destruction of people that God brought to pass in Noah's time. The earth itself was not destroyed. But the wicked were executed by a global flood. God preserved Noah and his family; they formed a righteous earthly society on a cleansed globe. After referring to that, Peter was inspired by God to foretell the coming of "the day of judgment and of destruction of the ungodly men." That will be followed by a "new heavens and a new earth" in which "righteousness is to dwell."—2 Peter 3:5-7, 13; Ecclesiastes 1:4; Isaiah 45:18.

[5] Naturally, we want to know when that destructive end of the present system of things will come. Jesus said that only the Father knows "that day and hour." (Matthew 24:36) But does that leave us completely in the dark? No, for God kindly put in his Word information so that his worshipers could know when the time was close.—Compare Amos 3:7.

According to the Bible, what is going to end? (4) Why can we be sure the "end" will come? (5, 6)

⁶ The Bible gives us reason for confidence in God's ability to forecast future developments. For example, in Daniel 9:24-27 he recorded a prophecy to indicate when the Messiah, or Christ, would arrive. First-century physician Luke relates that in 29 C.E. the Jews, knowing of Daniel's prophecy, were awaiting the Messiah. (Luke 3:1, 2, 15) Jewish scholar Abba Hillel Silver agrees, writing: "The Messiah was expected around the second quarter of the first century C.E." Jesus was baptized and became the Christ in 29 C.E., the very year indicated by Daniel's prophecy.

⁷ The same prophecy in Daniel foretold that after the Messiah's death, 'the city and the holy place would be brought to ruin.' Yes, God told in advance that Jerusalem and its holy temple were to be destroyed, ending the existing Jewish system of things.—Daniel 9:26.

⁸ Shortly before his death in 33 C.E., Jesus elaborated on this. He said that God was abandoning Jerusalem and her temple. Also, he said that he was going away, to return later. (Matthew 23:37–24:2) But his disciples asked:

"Tell us, When will these things be, and what will be the sign of your presence and of the conclusion of the system of things [or, 'end of the world']?"—Matthew 24:3.

⁹ His answer would have life-or-death importance to first-century Christians. It is just as important for us, because, as we will see, Jesus' reply had meaning beyond what the apostles asked about or could understand.—John 16:4, 12, 13.

¹⁰ Jesus referred to Daniel's prophecy. (Matthew

What did Jesus predict about the Jewish system of things? And what occurred? (7-10)

24:15) That had not pinpointed the year for Jerusalem's desolation, and neither would Jesus. But he described events to form a "sign" that the Jewish system was in its last days. You can read his words in Matthew 24:4-21 and Luke 21:10-24. He foretold false Messiahs (Christs), wars, food shortages, earthquakes, pestilences, persecution of Christians and an extensive preaching campaign. History bears out that those things occurred within the generation that survived until the Romans destroyed Jerusalem in 70 C.E.

FALSE CHRISTS: Josephus, a first-century historian, mentions three professed Messiahs
WARS: There were Parthian wars in southwest Asia; revolts in Gaul and Spain; uprisings of Jews in parts of the Empire; Syrian and Samaritan uprisings against the Jews
FAMINE: Famines occurred in Rome, Greece and Judea, one of which is reported on in Acts 11:28
EARTHQUAKES: These happened on Crete, in Smyrna, Hierapolis, Colossae, Chios, Miletus, Samos, Rome and Judea
CHRISTIANS WERE PERSECUTED but they PREACHED WIDELY: See the record in Acts 8:1, 14; 9:1, 2; 24:5; 28:22

[11] Because Christians trusted Jesus' prophecy they could take lifesaving action. Christ had warned: 'When you see Jerusalem surrounded by encamped armies, flee.' (Luke 21:20-24) As foretold, the Romans under General Gallus encircled Jerusalem in October of 66 C.E. How could Christians flee? Unexpectedly the armies withdrew. Christians, acting on Jesus' warning, fled the city. In 70 C.E., the Romans under General Titus returned. They desolated the city, killing over a million Jews. If you visit Rome, you can see a memorial of this carved on the Arch of Titus.

How important was it to understand the "sign"? (11, 12)

[12] What occurred during the last days of the Jewish system proves the absolute reliability of the "sign" Jesus gave. This is important to us because Jesus' prophecy about "the conclusion of the system of things" has even greater meaning today.

ANOTHER FULFILLMENT OF JESUS' PROPHECY

[13] What Jesus foretold about false Christs, wars, famines and earthquakes, and persecution of Christians, found fulfillment before 70 C.E. However, he predicted additional things that clearly were to come at a later time. He said that "all the

Why should we look for another fulfillment of the "sign," and how would it differ from the first fulfillment? (13-16)

Acting on Jesus' warning, Christians fled Jerusalem before the Romans destroyed it

tribes of the earth" would be forced to recognize his presence in heavenly glory. (Matthew 24:30) Also, he foretold that peoples would be separated as "sheep from the goats," and the sheeplike persons would enter into everlasting life. (Matthew 25:32, 46) Those things did not occur before or in 70 C.E.

¹⁴ Over 25 years after Jerusalem's fall, God moved the apostle John to write in Revelation about *future* events. In the sixth chapter, John foresaw "horsemen" who would bring disastrous things to the earth. You will see in reading Revelation 6:3-8 that John foretold (1) warfare, (2) "food shortage" and (3) "deadly plague." These are some of the very things Jesus had predicted in the "sign." Thus we have added proof that there was to be a second or larger fulfillment of what Jesus had foretold. Professor A. T. Robertson says on this:

"It is sufficient for our purpose to think of Jesus as using the destruction of the temple and of Jerusalem which did happen in that generation in A.D. 70, as also a symbol of his own second coming and of the end of the world or consummation of the age." —*Word Pictures in the New Testament*, Volume 1, page 188.

¹⁵ 'But,' some say, 'there have always been wars, famines and pestilences. So how does one recognize the second fulfillment of the "sign"?'

¹⁶ Obviously, it would have to be something outstanding, different from a local war, an isolated pestilence or a single earthquake. Note that Revelation 6:4 says that the warfare would "take peace away [not from one nation or region, but] from *the earth*." In addition, Jesus showed that it would be a *composite* sign. So, along with widespread war, there would be noteworthy famines,

earthquakes and plagues, to name a few. These would all come upon one generation. (Matthew 24:32-34) Appreciating this, and looking over human history, many persons discern clearly that the 'sign of the conclusion of the system of things' has now appeared.

THE "SIGN" IN OUR TIME

[17] Revelation 6:4 indicated that there would be earth-wide war. Has there been? Yes, beginning with the war of 1914-1918. Columnist Sydney J. Harris writes that 'World War I involved countries comprising more than 90 percent of the world's population.' According to the *Encyclopedia Americana,* over 8,000,000 soldiers were killed in World War I and more than 12,000,000 civilians died by massacre, starvation or exposure.

[18] Some try to dismiss this by saying that previously men just did not have the transportation and technology for *world* war. But that emphasizes the uniqueness of World War I.

"As time has passed since the days of August, 1914, it has become increasingly clear that the outbreak of the First World War meant the end of an age."—*The Norton History of Modern Europe.*

"World War I—simply The Great War to its survivors—remains the watershed of modern history in men's minds. . . . There is a kind of truth in the unconscious belief most people hold that Modern times began with World War I. It was the time when we lost our innocence."—Montreal *Gazette.*

"Nineteen-eighteen did not usher in the millennium, it ushered in a half century of conflict—turbulence, war, revolution, desolation, and ruin on a scale never before seen or even imagined."— Professor H. S. Commager.

How has the foretold warfare come to pass in our time? (17-19)

"War has never been easy to explain and World War I is perhaps the hardest of all. Beneath the dry accounts of rivalries and alliances which historians use to explain the war, there lies a sense of something far greater, a sense of restlessness troubling the world. . . . The war was hardly over when the world began preparing for the next."
—Barry Renfrew of Associated Press.

"The events set in motion on August 4, 1914 . . . destroyed a moral-cum-political order, broke up an international balance of power, ended Europe's role as the world's maker of events and killed, in the proceedings, several dozen million people. . . . in 1914 the world lost a coherence which it has not managed to recapture since."—London, "The Economist."

[19] Yes, 'war was ushered in on a scale never imagined,' just as the Bible had indicated. Soon there was a second *world* war costing between "35,000,000 and 60,000,000" lives.

"World War II spread death and devastation throughout most of the world to an extent never before experienced. . . . an attempt to express the value of property and livelihoods destroyed in terms of money is futile: the resulting sums reach astronomical figures."—*Encyclopedia Americana.*

And you know that aside from the many wars since 1945, we now have the threat of nuclear war.

[20] Unprecedented disease is another evidence that the major fulfillment of the "sign" began with World War I. (Luke 21:11) After acknowledging that earlier plagues killed large numbers

What fulfillment has occurred as to pestilence? (20)

over a period of decades, the magazine *Science Digest* showed how vastly greater was the Spanish influenza of 1918:

> "The war had killed over 21 million people in four years of dogged conflict; the influenza epidemic took approximately the same toll in about four months. In all history there had been no sterner, swifter visitation of death. . . . One doctor called it the medical catastrophe of all time."

> "The usual world figure is 21 million dead, but it is 'probably a gross underestimation.' That many may well have died on the Indian subcontinent alone; the mortality there in October of 1918 was 'without parallel in the history of disease.'"—*Scientific American.*

Nor have scientists halted the harvest of death by disease. When one disease seems "conquered," another gains. Men send rockets to the moon, but they have not overcome malaria, cancer and heart disease.

[21] Jesus said that "earthquakes in one place after another" would also be part of the "sign." (Matthew 24:7; Luke 21:11) There have been earthquakes throughout history. But how does the period since World War I compare? In *Il Piccolo,* Geo Malagoli observes:

> "Our generation lives in a dangerous period of high seismic activity, as statistics show. In fact, during a period of 1,059 years (from 856 to 1914) reliable sources list only 24 major earthquakes causing 1,973,000 deaths. However, [in] recent disasters, we find that 1,600,000 persons have died in only 63 years, as a result of 43 earthquakes which occurred from 1915 to 1978. This dramatic increase further goes to emphasize another accepted fact—our generation is an unfortunate one in many ways."

What other evidence could you point to, showing that the "sign" is being fulfilled? (21-23)

EARTHQUAKE DEATHS
(Estimation based on 1,122 years)

Up to 1914 — 1,800 a year

Since 1914 — 25,300 a year

[22] Persons may say that the growing world population and the size of cities account for the higher earthquake death toll since World War I. Even if this is the reason, it does not change what has happened. This is also true of famine. Despite advances in food production, such as the Green Revolution, we read news reports like these:

"At least one out of every eight people on earth is still afflicted by some form of malnutrition."

"The UN World Food Council convened in Ottawa this fall and confirmed that 50 million people starve to death each year."

"World food agencies estimate that more than one billion people won't get enough to eat this year."

[23] "Increasing of lawlessness" and a decline in love were also evidences to mark "the conclusion of the system of things." (Matthew 24:3, 12) You probably need no statistics on crime or terrorism to convince you that this is being fulfilled today. But, in this regard, read the prophetic description of the "last days" in 2 Timothy 3:1-5. See how accurately it fits what we face now.

WHAT DOES IT MEAN TO YOU?

[24] Jesus foretold that many persons would be distressed by the fulfillment of the "sign." "Men

What bearing does the current fulfillment of the "sign" have on your life? (24-26)

[will] become faint out of fear and expectation of the things coming upon the inhabited earth." However, it would be different with his followers. Christ told them: "As these things start to occur, raise yourselves erect and lift your heads up, because your *deliverance* is getting near." (Luke 21:26, 28) We must not ignore what is happening, nor senselessly brush it aside as coincidental. Those in Jerusalem who ignored the fulfillment of Jesus' prophecy in their day lost their lives. Jesus tells us: "Keep awake . . . that you may succeed in *escaping*."—Luke 21:34-36.

²⁵ Yes, it is possible to survive the end of the present wicked system of things. No human knows the exact "day and hour" of the coming end, but what has occurred on earth in our lifetime proves that it is very near. However, more is asked of us than merely 'keeping on the watch.' (Matthew 24:36-42) It should have an effect on our thinking and conduct. Peter writes: "Your lives should be holy and dedicated to God, as you wait for the Day of God. . . . Do your best to be pure and faultless."—2 Peter 3:11-14, *Good News Bible*.

²⁶ As part of the "sign," Jesus said: "This good news of the kingdom will be preached in all the inhabited earth for a witness to all the nations; and then the end will come." (Matthew 24:14) To have our proper share in that activity, we need to know what that "kingdom" is and why it is so vital now since the end is near. Let us now examine this.

16

A Government to Bring
Earth-wide Peace

IS THERE any government that is able to bring lasting peace to earth? that can provide security and freedom from crime? that can make available an abundance of good food for all? that is able to clean up the environment and overcome disease?

[2] Consider man's record in the field of government—monarchies, democracies and socialistic or Communistic rules. None of these, nor all of them together, have been able to do the fine things just mentioned; not even on a small scale, to say nothing of earth wide. Nevertheless, there is reason for you to have hope.

POINT FOR DISCUSSION: What desirable things have human governments been unable to accomplish? (1, 2)

"The failure to create a genuine basis for world peace . . . is directly chargeable to the refusal of nations, especially the larger ones, to accept an authority that can tell them what to do in the international arena.

"This, then, is the basic challenge today—how to create a world authority to keep the peace that has behind it the confidence of the world's peoples."—Editor Norman Cousins, "Saturday Review."

GOD PURPOSES A GOVERNMENT—THE KINGDOM

³ Jehovah God himself promises to supply what we need. How can we be sure of that? Remember that he originally purposed a global paradise in which people could enjoy peace and happiness. (Genesis 1:28; 2:8, 9) Then rebellion occurred in the garden of Eden. But do you think that God would allow unappreciative creatures to defeat his purpose? Absolutely not. In fact, soon after Adam and Eve rebelled, Jehovah foretold a coming deliverer, a "seed" who would crush peace disturbers in heaven and on earth. (Genesis 3:15) 'But,' you may wonder, 'where does "government" come into the picture?' That "seed" was to be the Messiah, the Prince of Peace, about whom the prophet Isaiah was inspired to write: "To the abundance of [his] *princely rule* and to peace there will be no end."—Isaiah 9:6, 7; 11:1-5.

⁴ Yes, the promise of Jehovah is for a rulership that will administer justice and bring peace. The Bible calls this rulership the kingdom of God. Millions have prayed: "Our Father . . . let your kingdom come." (Matthew 6:9, 10) If you have offered this prayer, you have been praying for a real government—the heavenly kingdom—which will bring peace to earth. (Psalm 72:1-8) But when would God put that government into operation? How would he select and qualify its rulers?

⁵ Over the centuries God's purpose unfolded. For example, he showed that the Messiah would come through Abraham, through Jacob, and would be of the tribe of Judah. (Genesis 22:18;

How do we know that God purposes a government that will bring peace? (3, 4)

What steps did God take toward producing the Kingdom? (5, 6)

9:10) Then Jehovah established over Israel a
kingdom that was a prophetic pattern of things
to come. Israel was a theocracy (God-rule). Their
king was said to sit on "Jehovah's throne."
(1 Chronicles 29:23) Jehovah was the ultimate
authority; his laws and standards guided the nation. In time, God told King David that through
his family would come one who would be a
permanent king.—Psalm 89:20, 21, 29.

⁶ Such details and other Bible information about
Israelite history are important because they show
us that God was laying a secure legal foundation
for the coming kingdom. In harmony with this,
God later sent an angel to a virgin girl of the
house of David to tell her:

"You will . . . give birth to a son, and you are to
call his name Jesus. This one will be great and
will be called Son of the Most High; and Jehovah
God will give him the throne of David his father,
and he will rule as king over the house of Jacob
forever, and there will be no end of his kingdom."
—Luke 1:28-33.

⁷ This is the foretold Messiah, the one to whom
God promised to give lasting rulership over humankind. What can we expect from Jesus as
ruler? Let us examine some of his record.

⁸ Jesus has always been fully devoted to God
and the doing of His will. (Hebrews 10:9; Isaiah
11:3) One way in which he showed his loyalty
to God was by refusing bribes of wealth or prominence, quite in contrast to many human rulers.
(Luke 4:5-8) He was fearless in upholding the
truth, so he did not hold back from exposing religious hypocrisy.—John 2:13-17; Mark 7:1-13.

Why can we be sure that Jesus will be an outstanding
ruler? (7-10)

⁹ Christ also has outstanding love for mankind as demonstrated by the fact that he gave his life in our behalf. (John 13:34; 15:12, 13) Moved with compassion, Jesus cured the sick, raised the dead and provided food for the needy. (Luke 7: 11-15, 22; 9:11-17) He also has power over natural forces and used it to benefit people. (Matthew 8:23-27) Yet he is approachable; even children were at ease with this mild-tempered man —Matthew 11:28-30; 19:13-15.

¹⁰ Imagine the blessing of having him as Ruler with his qualities and abilities! That is the grand prospect Jehovah's worshipers have.

RULERSHIP FROM HEAVEN

¹¹ When a Roman governor asked Jesus about his kingship, he replied: "My kingdom is no part of this world." (John 18:36) Jesus kept strictly neutral as to the politics of the nations, setting an example for his followers. (John 6:15; 2 Corinthians 5:20) Furthermore, it was not God's purpose for his Son to rule from an earthly location. He was to rule from heaven, where he could exercise superhuman, universal authority.

¹² With that prospect in view, after Jesus had died faithful to God, his Father raised him to life as an immortal spirit creature. (Acts 10:39-43; 1 Corinthians 15:45) Christ appeared to his followers and assured them that he was alive and active. Then Jesus ascended to heaven. Concerning this, the apostle Peter wrote: "He is at God's right hand, for he went his way to heaven; and angels and authorities and powers were made subject to him."—1 Peter 3:22; Matthew 28:18.

What reasons are there to know that Jesus is not to rule on earth? (11, 12)

[13] Starting at that time, in 33 C.E., Christ began ruling over the Christian congregation, and his followers happily acknowledged his lordship and heavenly position. (Colossians 1:13, 14) Yet it was not God's purpose for Jesus to begin ruling over the world of mankind and the universe then.

[14] God was permitting men time to see for themselves the fruits of human rulership. Hence, Christ had to wait until the appointed time for Kingdom rule over the world. The apostle Paul wrote: "This man offered one sacrifice for sins perpetually and sat down at the right hand of God, from then on awaiting until his enemies should be placed as a stool for his feet."—Hebrews 10:12, 13.

[15] But if Jesus is invisible in heaven, how can we know when the time comes for him to begin ruling? As discussed in the previous chapter, Jesus gave a visible "sign" so that his followers on earth would know when that time had arrived. (Matthew 24:3-31) The wars, famines, earthquakes, persecution of Christians and global preaching of the Kingdom good news that we have seen since World War I (1914-1918) confirm that we are living in the conclusion of the system of things. These events also prove that Christ is now ruling in heaven, for, after describing a war in heaven against Satan, the Bible says:

"Now have come to pass the salvation and the power and the kingdom of our God and the authority of his Christ. . . . On this account be glad, you heavens and you who reside in them! Woe for the earth and for the sea, because the Devil has come down to you, having great anger, knowing he has a short period of time."—Revelation 12:7-12.

[16] Hence, Jesus Christ is now reigning. This

What evidence is there as to when Christ began ruling over mankind? (13-16)

means that it will be only a "short period of time" until he exerts his authority to eliminate all opposition to the Kingdom, including the Devil and all man-made governments. (Daniel 2:44) Then we will be able to rejoice in a theocratic kingdom that will bring lasting peace.

CORULERS IN THE KINGDOM

[17] Another fascinating aspect of the Kingdom is disclosed in the Bible. Daniel 7:13, 14 gives us a description of God's Son receiving "rulership and dignity and kingdom." Then the vision says:

> "The kingdom and the rulership and the grandeur of the kingdoms under all the heavens were given to the *people who are the holy ones of the Supreme One*. Their kingdom is an indefinitely lasting kingdom, and all the rulerships will serve and obey even them."—Daniel 7:27.

So God purposes for Jesus Christ to have associate rulers. That means that some humans will go to heaven. When Jesus was on earth he began selecting men and women to become corulers with him. He said that he was going to heaven to prepare a place for them.—John 14:1-3.

[18] This helps to clear up something that many who have attended church all their life do not understand: On the one hand, the Bible shows that God purposed for humans to live on earth; yet, on the other hand, the Bible talks about humans going to heaven. How does this work out? Well, God has promised to take some humans to heaven to be with his Son in the Kingdom government. But the earth is going to be a paradise filled with happy, peaceful humans.—See Psalm 37:29; Isaiah 65:17, 20-25.

Who will rule with Jesus in the Kingdom? (17, 18)

¹⁹ How many will go to heaven as part of the Kingdom government? Jesus gave indication, saying: "Have no fear, *little flock,* because your Father has approved of giving you the kingdom." (Luke 12:32) Yes, the number is limited. Revelation shows that those "bought from among mankind" to reign with "the Lamb" (Jesus Christ) number 144,000. (Revelation 14:1-5) That is not hard to understand. Even some human governments have a selected body of men and women who go to the capital as part of the government.

²⁰ But God has not left it up to humans to determine who will go to heaven. He selects them. (1 Peter 2:4, 5, 9; Romans 8:28-30; 9:16) When God chose the apostle Paul, he poured out his spirit on him, giving Paul the conviction that he would be part of the "heavenly kingdom." (2 Timothy 4:18) Paul wrote: "The spirit itself bears witness with our spirit that we are God's children. If, then, we are children, we are also heirs: heirs indeed of God, but joint heirs with Christ."—Romans 8:16, 17; 2 Corinthians 1:22; 5:5.

²¹ Relatively few of God's worshipers have been chosen for life in heaven, since God's purpose was for humans to live in happiness on earth. Jesus was the first one taken to heaven. (Hebrews 6:19, 20; Matthew 11:11) Thereafter God continued selecting 144,000 others. What would happen when that number was complete?

²² After being given a vision of the limited number (144,000) in heaven with Christ, the apostle John was shown "a great crowd, which no man was able to number." (Revelation 7:4, 9, 10) These will be protected by God through the de-

---

How many will go to heaven, and why not all mankind? (19-22)

structive end of the present system of things
They have the wonderful prospect of everlasting
life on earth, the same prospect that applies to
men of faith such as Noah, Abraham and David
who died before God opened the way to heavenly
life for the 144,000.—Acts 2:34.

REASONS FOR CONFIDENCE IN THE RULERS

[23] Today most persons have little confidence in
their rulers. However, those who will rule in God's
kingdom are very different from worldly rulers.
Over the centuries God has chosen persons who
have proved their faith. Under all sorts of trials
and temptations, they have adhered to what is
right and just. They gain God's confidence, so
can we not have confidence in them?

[24] Also, their having been humans will enable
them to understand and sympathize with us.
(Compare Hebrews 4:15, 16.) They know what
it means to be tired, worried, discouraged. They
know the effort needed to become more patient,
kind and merciful. And some of them were wom-
en; they understand the feelings and special needs
of women on earth.—Galatians 3:28.

[25] Millions of Jehovah's Witnesses today are
proving their confidence in Christ and his corulers, and are showing how real the Kingdom
is to them. They do this by being *loyal subjects*
of God's kingdom. (Proverbs 14:28) They accept
and recommend its *laws* written in the Bible,
truly believing that Christianity is the best way
of life. They share in this government's *educational program*. The Bible is the main textbook,

---

What reasons do we have for confidence in these corulers? (23, 24)
How can we show our support for the Kingdom? (25-27)

REALISTIC ABOUT GOVERNMENT

"Our weapons were cudgels, lead-lined clubs, chains and guns," relates Stelvio, who in the 1970's was a political activist in southern Europe. At clandestine military-like camps he had learned how to organize mobs and carry on city warfare.

But after some years a change came. One of Jehovah's Witnesses visited Stelvio's home, teaching the Bible. The effect? "It opened my eyes to see that nationalism and political factions divide men. I learned from the Bible that God made out of one man every nation of men, to dwell upon the earth. (Acts 17:26) This realization is a unifying force. It freed me of hating others just because their political ideas were different."

This formerly violent activist adds: "I keep asking myself: How can man ever resolve his problems by politics, since politics itself has caused divisions of mankind? For men to get together, the reasons for divisions must disappear. I have seen among Jehovah's Witnesses blacks and whites getting baptized in the same water, former Protestants and Catholics in Ireland stop hating one another, Arabs and Jews meeting together during the Six-Day War. I have learned to love those that I had hated.

"Nobody can say that God's kingdom, which Jehovah's Witnesses long for, is a mere utopian dream, because there is already an international community united under that kingdom. Applying Bible principles has brought results that no other religious, political or social group has achieved.

"To those who, like me in the past, struggle to bring justice, peace and social order, I say: 'Be realistic and admit that man has been unable to bring them. Look, though, at Jehovah's Witnesses. Have they not overcome problems with war, political divisions, racial discrimination, peace and unity? Men trust in men and have problems. Jehovah's Witnesses submit to God's kingdom and have resolved the main problems of living.'"

used along with Christian reference works and study aids. At congregational meetings they learn more about the Kingdom and Christian living. And they carry the educational program to others by teaching publicly and in homes.—Acts 20:20.

²⁶ Jesus said that one feature of the sign of the "last days" would be: "This good news of the kingdom will be preached in all the inhabited earth for a witness to all the nations; and then the end will come." (Matthew 24:14) Before Jesus ascended to heaven he emphasized the need for his disciples to have an active share in this evangelizing work.—Matthew 28:19, 20; Acts 1:8.

²⁷ Christians today realize that sharing in this preaching and teaching work is an important way that they can demonstrate their love for God and for their neighbors. (Mark 12:28-31) Lives are involved, so it is a serious responsibility. (Acts 20:26, 27; 1 Corinthians 9:16) It is also a source of considerable happiness and satisfaction. (Acts 20:35) Jehovah's Witnesses will be glad to help you to teach others about God's ruling kingdom.

17

Whose Laws Will You Put First?

WE LIVE with law—laws of nature, or creation; laws from God on morals and conduct; secular laws. We easily accept and benefit from many of these. But what if a law seems unduly restrictive? Or if there is a conflict between two laws affecting you?

² Since natural laws seem rather impersonal, few individuals have problems in accepting them. Who would defy the law of gravity by walking off a high cliff? And that law benefits us; it keeps our feet on the ground and the food on our plate. Other natural laws involve genetics, which affect what our children will be like. By being conscious of genetic laws and not marrying a close relative, we avoid the danger of passing on to our children certain defects. (Compare Leviticus 18:6-17.) But what about laws on conduct or morals?

³ Many persons develop a resentment toward legislated laws. One reason is that humans have tended to make needless laws and to oppress others by means of laws. (Matthew 15:2; 23:4) However, there is danger in viewing all laws as bad or in making it a practice to ignore them.

⁴ Mankind's dying condition can be traced to a rebellion against law. God forbade Adam and Eve to eat from the tree of the knowledge of good

POINT FOR DISCUSSION: Why should we give thought to how we will view laws? (1-4)

and bad. But Satan suggested to Eve that God's law was unduly restrictive. (Genesis 3:1-6) Satan's appeal was—'No rules. Set your own standards.' That anti-law spirit has been popular down through history, even until today.

⁵ Jehovah does not oppress his people with needlessly inhibiting or burdensome laws, for "where the spirit of Jehovah is, there is freedom." (2 Corinthians 3:17; James 1:25) Yet, contrary to what Satan wants people to believe, Jehovah is the Sovereign Ruler of the universe. He is its Creator as well as being our Life-Giver and Provider. (Acts 4:24; 14:15-17) So he has the right to direct us and make laws as to our conduct.

⁶ Many persons agree that, as the ultimate authority, God has the right to decree what humans can and can not do. That is, they agree until they strongly want to do something that God forbids. Obviously, that is dangerous. There is ample proof that God's commands are for our good. For example, avoiding drunkenness, wrath and covetousness will help us to enjoy better health and to have more contentment. (Psalm 119:1-9, 105) Also, God's laws can help us to gain his approval and salvation. (Proverbs 21:30, 31) So even if persons do not yet understand the reason behind some of Jehovah's commands, for them to refuse to obey, perhaps because of prideful independence, is folly.

⁷ An example of God's commands for Christians is a decree issued by a council of the apostles and older men in Jerusalem, who formed a governing body of the early Christian congregation:

What do we need to recognize about God's laws? (5, 6)
What reasons do we have to obey God's law against "fornication"? (7, 8)

"The holy spirit and we ourselves have favored adding no further burden to you, except these necessary things, to keep abstaining from things sacrificed to idols and from blood and from things strangled and from fornication."—Acts 15:22-29.

⁸ We have sound reasons to obey God's law on "fornication"—protection against disease, illegitimacy, broken marriages. That law means that people are not to engage in homosexuality or other gross sexual immorality, all of which are covered by the Greek word *porneia* (fornication) used in Acts 15:29. (Romans 1:24-27, 32) But what if the *dangers* of "fornication" could be avoided? Would we still obey God's command *because he is our Sovereign Ruler?* If we do, we help to prove that Satan is a liar, that humans will obey Jehovah because they love him.—Job 2:3-5; 27:5; Psalm 26:1, 11.

⁹ That decree set out in Acts 15:22-29 identifies another area in which we can show our obedience. It is God's command to 'abstain from blood' and from the meat of animals strangled to keep blood in them. God told our ancestor Noah that humans may eat animal flesh, but must not sustain their lives with the blood of another creature. (Genesis 9:3-6) When repeating this law to the Israelites, God said that "the soul [or, life] of the flesh is in the blood." The only way they were to use blood was on the altar to atone for sin. Otherwise, blood from a creature was to be poured out, figuratively returning it to God. Obeying this law meant life or death.—Leviticus 17:10-14.

¹⁰ Those sacrifices pictured the pouring out of Jesus' blood in our behalf. (Ephesians 1:7; Revelation 1:5; Hebrews 9:12, 23-28) Even after

How can we obey God's law about blood? (9-11)

Christ returned to heaven, God commanded Christians to 'abstain from blood.' But how many persons claiming to be Christians obey the Divine Lawgiver and Life-Giver in this matter? In some places it is common for persons to include among the foods they eat unbled meat, blood sausage or other food deliberately containing blood.

[11] Similarly, many persons have accepted blood transfusions in an effort to live longer. Often they are unaware that blood transfusions themselves pose serious health risks and that virtually any type of surgery can be done without blood by employing alternative therapies.* But even if it seemed life were at stake, would it be a mistake to obey God? Divine law must not be ignored even in an emergency.—1 Samuel 14:31-35.

[12] In upholding their belief in freedom of speech or worship, or some political ideal, many men have risked death. They have obeyed a ruler or a military commander no matter what the danger. Do we not have much more compelling reasons to obey the Sovereign of the universe? 'Absolutely,' answers the record of integrity set by many men of faith. (Daniel 3:8-18; Hebrews 11:35-38) They knew, as we should, that Jehovah is the Life-Giver and will remember and reward those obeying him—if necessary restoring them to life by means of a resurrection in his due time. (Hebrews 5:9; 6:10; John 11:25) We can be sure that, under any circumstance, obeying Jehovah is the right and lastingly best course.—Mark 8:35.

---

* Religious, ethical and medical aspects of this are presented in the booklet *Jehovah's Witnesses and the Question of Blood,* published by the Watchtower Bible and Tract Society.

Why should we obey God even if our life is threatened? (12)

Your taxes pay for . . .

Police Protection

Sanitation

Education

Mail Delivery

Water Distribution

Fire Fighting

OBEY GOVERNMENTAL LAWS?

¹³ Many other laws affecting us daily come from secular governments. How should the Christian view and react to these laws? The apostle Paul wrote: "Remind people to be loyally subject to the government and its officials, to obey the laws."—Titus 3:1, *The New American Bible*.

¹⁴ In the first century C.E., the Roman government was not always just, and some of its rulers were immoral and dishonest. Yet Paul said: "Let every soul be in subjection to the superior authorities, for there is no authority except by God." The "superior authorities" are the existing secular governments.—Romans 13:1.

¹⁵ Jehovah acknowledges that until his rule is fully restored to earth, civil governments serve some useful purposes. They help to keep a measure of order in society and provide numerous services, including the registering of marriages and births. (Compare Luke 2:1-5.) Thus Christians generally can "go on leading a calm and quiet life with full godly devotion and seriousness."—1 Timothy 2:2.

¹⁶ While awaiting the time when God's kingdom will solve the problems of war, injustice and oppres-

How should Christians view secular governments, and why? (Matthew 22: 19-21) (13-16)

sion, Christians are not to 'oppose the authority' of civil governments. They are to pay the required taxes honestly, obey the laws and give respect to rulers. For this course true Christians have often been praised and helped by officials, and they seldom are punished with "the sword" used against lawbreakers.—Romans 13:2-7.

BEING IN RELATIVE SUBJECTION

[17] Sometimes there is a conflict between laws. A civil government may require something that God forbids. Or civil law may forbid a thing that God commands Christians to do. What then?

[18] Such a conflict occurred when rulers forbade the apostles to preach about the resurrected Jesus Christ. Read the faith-strengthening account at Acts 4:1-23; 5:12-42. Though imprisoned and flogged, the apostles would not stop preaching. Peter said: "We must obey God as ruler rather than men."—Acts 5:29.

[19] So a Christian's subjection to the governmental authorities is a *relative* subjection. His first obligation is to obey the Supreme Authority. If, as a result, he suffers punishment, he can gain comfort in knowing that God approves of what he is doing.—1 Peter 2:20-23.

[20] The early Christians faced decisions in another area involving what God directed and what the Roman government expected. This had to do with supporting or being in the Roman army. God had said of his people: "They will have to beat their swords into plowshares and their spears into pruning shears. Nation will not lift up sword against nation, neither will they learn war anymore." (Isaiah 2:4; Matthew 26:52) If, then, the

What is the right course when God's law and secular laws conflict? Illustrate. (17-21)

Roman government demanded that a Christian be in its army or support its war efforts, there would be a conflict between Caesar's law and God's.

"A careful review of all the information available goes to show that, until the time of Marcus Aurelius [emperor from 161 to 180 C.E.], no Christian became a soldier; and no soldier, after becoming a Christian, remained in military service."—"The Rise of Christianity."

---

[21] Early Christians also put God's law first when they were ordered by men to offer incense to the deity of Rome's Caesar. Others may have thought the act to be patriotic. But history tells us that Christians saw it as a form of idolatry. They would not perform idolatrous acts toward any person or object, knowing that their devotion belonged to Jehovah. (Matthew 22:21; 1 John 5:21) And rather than get involved in politics, even by shouting idolatrous praise to a ruler, they kept neutral so as to be "no part of the world," as Jesus had urged.—John 15:19; Acts 12:21-23.

[22] Will you accept God's thinking and his directions on the matter of law? Doing so will protect you from many sorrows experienced by persons who disregard God's laws on conduct and morals. And you will not experience needless punishment from existing civil authorities. But God's thinking on the matter includes, above all, recognizing him as the Supreme Ruler. If you will do that under all circumstances, then you will fit in when the laws of God's kingdom will soon prevail over the entire earth.—Daniel 7:27.

What test do we now face? (22)

18

Is There Good in All Religions?

WHEN religion is discussed, many persons say, 'There's good in all religions,' or, 'All religions are just different roads leading to God.'

² It is easy to see why persons might find some good in almost any religion, for most of them speak about love and teach that murder, stealing and lying are wrong. Religious groups have sent out missionaries to run hospitals and help the poor. And especially in the last two centuries they have shared in translating and distributing the Bible, thus allowing more persons to benefit from God's Word. (2 Timothy 3:16) Yet we owe it to ourselves to ask: How do Jehovah and Jesus Christ view the different religions?

THE RIGHT WAY—A NARROW WAY

³ Some persons who feel there is good in all religions consider it narrow-minded to believe that God would not accept most people no matter what their religion. But Jesus, who knew and reflected his Father's thinking, took a different view. (John 1:18; 8:28, 29) None of us would reasonably charge the Son of God with being narrow-minded. Consider what he said in the Sermon on the Mount:

POINT FOR DISCUSSION: Why should we consider whether there is good in all religions? (1, 2)
What was Jesus' view of religion, and why? (3-5)

"Go in through the narrow gate; because broad and spacious is the road leading off into destruction, and many are the ones going in through it; whereas narrow is the gate and cramped the road leading off into life, and few are the ones finding it."—Matthew 7:13, 14.

[4] What does it take to be on that narrow road and have God's approval? Some, in line with the modern liberal or ecumenical spirit, would answer, 'Just do good and avoid hurting others,' or, 'All you need is to accept Jesus as your Lord.' But Jesus said that much more is necessary:

"Not everyone saying to me, 'Lord, Lord,' will enter into the kingdom of the heavens, but the one DOING THE WILL OF MY FATHER who is in the heavens will. Many will say to me in that day, 'Lord, Lord, did we not . . . perform many powerful works in your name?' And yet then I will confess to them: I never knew you! Get away from me, you workers of lawlessness."—Matthew 7:21-23.

[5] It is true that Jesus counseled against judging the inconsequential faults of others. (Matthew 7:3-5; Romans 14:1-4) But on the vital matter of religion, he exemplified the need to adhere to the Bible, and to do the will of the Father. Jesus condemned practices and teachings that conflicted with God's Word. Why? Because he knew that religion is used by the Devil to ensnare people. (2 Corinthians 4:4) Satan's stock in trade is falsehood, but presented in a way that makes it appealing. (Genesis 3:4, 5; 1 Timothy 4:1-3) Even among professing Christians there are religious leaders who serve the desires of the Devil. (2 Corinthians 11:13-15) Their teachings misrepresent the loving and generous ways of Jehovah. Is it any wonder, then, that Jesus exposed religious

leaders whose teachings were contrary to the Scriptures?—Matthew 15:1-20; 23:1-38.

⁶ Many persons have, as it were, inherited their religion. Others just go along with the majority around them. But even if this is with sincerity, it can put a person on the 'broad road leading to destruction.' (John 16:2; Proverbs 16:25) The apostle Paul (also named Saul) had been zealous in his religion even to the point of persecuting Christians. Yet to be acceptable to God, he had to convert to a new way of worship. (1 Timothy 1:12-16; Acts 8:1-3; 9:1, 2) Later, he was inspired to write that some very religious persons then had "a zeal for God; but not according to accurate knowledge." (Romans 10:2) Do you have an accurate knowledge of the will of God set out in the Bible? Are you acting accordingly?

⁷ Do not take this lightly, perhaps feeling that if you are not quite on the right path God will understand without your having to make any changes. The Scriptures state that God's will is for people to "come to an accurate knowledge of truth," and then to live in harmony with it. (1 Timothy 2:3, 4; James 4:17) God foretold that in the "last days" many persons would 'have a form of godly devotion but prove false to its power.' He commanded: "From these turn away." —2 Timothy 3:1-5.

HOW CAN YOU KNOW?

⁸ Although worship that pleases God must accord with "accurate knowledge," examination reveals that most churches teach doctrines that

Why is it important that we have accurate knowledge? (6, 7)

How do some common teachings and practices conflict with the Bible? (8-11)

conflict with the Bible. (Romans 10:2) For example, they hold to the unscriptural doctrine that man has an immortal soul. (Ezekiel 18:4, 20; see page 115.) 'Is that teaching so bad?' some may wonder. Do not forget that Satan's first lie was that sin would not bring death. (Genesis 3:1-4) While death is now unavoidable, the teaching that man has an immortal soul tends to further Satan's lie. It has led millions of persons into fearful dealings with demons who pose as the souls of the dead. And the doctrine makes the Bible truth about a coming resurrection of the dead meaningless.—Acts 24:15.

⁹ Conduct is also involved, for many religions accept or encourage holidays and customs based on belief in immortality of the soul. Halloween, All Souls' Day and others are holidays of that sort, blending in practices drawn from non-Christian religions.

¹⁰ The mixing of non-Christian and supposed Christian religion extends to other holidays, such as Christmas. God directed Christians to commemorate Jesus' *death,* not his birth. (1 Corinthians 11:24-26) And the Bible shows that Jesus was not born in December, which is a cold rainy season in Israel. (Luke 2:8-11) You can check almost any encyclopedia and see that December 25 was chosen because it was already a Roman holiday. Sir James Frazer observes:

"Taken altogether, the coincidences of [Christmas and Easter] with the heathen festivals are too close and too numerous to be accidental. . . . [Clerics] perceived that if Christianity was to conquer the world it could do so only by relaxing the too rigid principles of its Founder, by widening a little the narrow gate which leads to salvation."—*The Golden Bough.*

[11] After he learns the facts, what person who sincerely loves Jehovah would continue to accept beliefs and practices based on a compromise with pagan worship? To some persons these teachings or practices may seem like little things. But the Bible clearly says: "A little leaven ferments the whole lump."—Galatians 5:9.

WAR AND MORALS

[12] Jesus Christ set out another aid in identifying religion that is acceptable to Jehovah when he told his disciples: "By this all will know that you are my disciples, if you have love among yourselves." (John 13:34, 35) Most churches talk about showing love, but do they really urge showing the kind of love that Jesus did?

[13] We have already seen that Christians in early centuries lived in line with the prophetic description at Isaiah 2:4. They 'beat their swords into plowshares and would not lift up sword against each other nor learn war anymore.' (See pages 166, 167.) What position have the churches and their clergy taken? Many men know from personal experience that the churches have approved of and blessed warfare—Catholics killing Catholics, Protestants killing Protestants. This certainly was not following the pattern Jesus set. Interestingly, it was the Jewish religious leaders who, claiming that national interests were at stake, approved of killing Jesus.—John 11:47-50; 15:17-19; 18:36.

[14] As a further aid in determining whether a

How do the churches and real Christianity compare on the matter of war? (12, 13)

True Christianity takes what position on holding to God's moral standards? (14-16)

"VALUES AND VIOLENCE IN AUSCHWITZ"

In her book of that title, Polish sociologist Anna Pawelczynska observed that in Nazi Germany "Jehovah's Witnesses waged passive resistance for their belief, which opposed all war and violence." With what result? She explains:

"This little group of prisoners was a solid ideological force and they won their battle against Nazism. The German group of this sect had been a tiny island of unflagging resistance existing in the bosom of a terrorized nation, and in that same undismayed spirit they functioned in the camp at Auschwitz. They managed to win the respect of their fellow-prisoners . . . of prisoner-functionaries, and even of the SS officers. Everyone knew that no Jehovah's Witness would perform a command contrary to his religious belief."

religious group has God's approval, consider whether it upholds his moral standards rather than simply overlooking wrongdoing. Jesus tried to help sin-laden persons, including drunkards and harlots. His disciples were to do the same. (Matthew 9:10-13; 21:31, 32; Luke 7:36-48; 15:1-32) And if a person who had already become a Christian sinned, other Christians could help him, trying to restore him to God's favor and to spiritual strength. (Galatians 6:1; James 5:13-16) But what if a person unrepentantly practiced sin?

¹⁵ That was true of a man in Corinth. Paul wrote:

"Quit mixing in company with anyone called a brother that is a fornicator or a greedy person or an idolater or a reviler or a drunkard or an extortioner, not even eating with such a man. . . . 'Remove the wicked man from among yourselves.'"—1 Corinthians 5:11-13.

Jehovah's Witnesses follow God's directions in this. If a gross sinner refuses to accept help and will not abandon his immoral way, such a person must be expelled or disfellowshiped from the congregation. Perhaps this will shock him to his senses. Yet, whether that happens or not, this course serves to protect the sincere members of the congregation who, though themselves imperfect, are striving to uphold God's standards.—1 Corinthians 5:1-8; 2 John 9-11.

[16] However, you may know of churchgoers who openly practice sin, perhaps even receiving special honors in their church because of their wealth or prominence. By refusing to follow God's command to disfellowship unrepentant sinners, the churches cause others to think they might as well sin too. (Ecclesiastes 8:11; 1 Corinthians 15:33) God cannot approve of those who produce such fruitage. —Matthew 7:15-20; Revelation 18:4-8.

STAYING ON THE ROAD TO LIFE

[17] Once you find the "road leading off into life," you need to keep on studying the Bible in order to stay on it. Try to read the Bible each day; form a longing for it. (1 Peter 2:2, 3; Matthew 4:4) It will equip you for "every good work."—2 Timothy 3:16, 17.

[18] Those good works include living by God's moral standards, as well as being kind and helpful to others, especially those related to us in the faith. (James 1:27; Galatians 6:9, 10) That is how Jesus was. Besides setting a fine moral example, he healed the sick, fed the hungry and comforted the distressed. He especially taught and strengthened his disciples. Though we can-

How can you stay on the road to life? (17, 18)

not copy his miracles, we can, as we are able, give practical aid to others, which may move some to glorify God.—1 Peter 2:12.

[19] But Jesus' good works involved more. He knew that the best work done for others was helping them to know what worship is acceptable to God and instructing them about God's Kingdom purposes. This could help them to attain the goal of everlasting life in happiness.—Luke 4:18-21.

[20] Christians today should likewise strive to be witnesses for Jehovah. They can witness by their fine conduct, which includes helping others and keeping themselves "without spot from the world." (Isaiah 43:10-12; James 1:27; Titus 2:14) Also, they can take the "good news" right to the homes of persons, persevering in this work until God says that it is done. (Luke 10:1-9) Do you not want to help your neighbors, including your family, to learn about worship that Jehovah accepts? Then you, too, should share in the public expression of your faith; doing so can help others to find the road to life.—Romans 10:10-15.

What additional work is vital for Christians? (19, 20)

Are you on the broad way . . .

. . . or the narrow way?

19

Will You Worship God in HIS Way?

IN THE "last days," the Bible foretells, men would "be lovers of themselves, . . . self-assuming, haughty, . . . having a form of godly devotion but proving false to its power." (2 Timothy 3:1-5) Does that not well describe what we see around us today?

² Yes, in every aspect of life people act in a way that says, "Me first"—their conduct when shopping or driving, the attention they give to clothing and makeup, and the type of dancing they do. But all of this has not brought real happiness.

³ Many people even view religion according to what *they* want or feel *they* need. What a mistake that is! We are not the ones to say how God should be worshiped. As the Creator and Life-Giver, Jehovah is the one to say how he should be worshiped. (Romans 9:20, 21) And what he requires of us is for our own good. It brings contentment now and keeps our mind and heart on the wonderful things that he has in store for us in the future.—Isaiah 48:17.

⁴ Jehovah does not burden Christians with needless ceremonies or impose pointless restrictions. But God knows that continued life depends on a good relationship with him, and that we need to

POINT FOR DISCUSSION: Who comes first with most people, and why is that not wise? (1-4)

live by his standards and show concern for others if we are to find true enjoyment in life. When we worship God the way *he* wants, life becomes richer and gains meaning.

DOING THINGS IN GOD'S WAY

⁵ Noah is a fine example of a person who complied with God's way. The Bible says: "Noah was a righteous man. He proved himself faultless among his contemporaries. Noah walked with the true God." After God gave him instructions to build a huge life-preserving ark, "Noah proceeded to do according to all that God had commanded him. He did just so." (Genesis 6:9, 22) Doing things in God's way saved Noah's life, as well as the lives of his family, who stuck with him as God's prophet on earth.—2 Peter 2:5.

⁶ Another person who followed God's way was Abraham. God told him to leave his homeland. Would you have obeyed? Abraham "went just as Jehovah had spoken," though "not knowing where he was going." (Genesis 12:4; Hebrews 11:8) Because of faithfully doing things in God's way, Abraham was counted as "Jehovah's friend." —James 2:23; Romans 4:11.

BEING AMONG GOD'S PEOPLE

⁷ In time God chose to deal with a large group, the nation of Israel. They became "his people, a special property, out of all the peoples who are on the surface of the ground." (Deuteronomy 14:2) Of course, each Israelite needed to pray to God and have a close, personal relationship with

How were Noah and Abraham different from most persons today? (5, 6)

In the time of ancient Israel, how did God deal with persons? (7-9)

him. But they also had to recognize that God was directing a congregation; they had to follow the form of worship outlined in God's law for them as a people. Thus they could enjoy the protection and blessing God provided for the congregation. (Deuteronomy 28:9-14) Think what a privilege it was to be part of those whom the Almighty called "my people Israel."—2 Samuel 7:8.

[8] What of non-Israelites who wanted to worship the true God? Persons of that sort formed "a vast mixed company" who chose to go with Israel when Moses led the nation out of Egypt. (Exodus 12:38) Had you been in Egypt, would you have felt that you could remain and worship God alone in your own way?

[9] Even when Israel settled in the Promised Land, foreigners who recognized Jehovah and wanted to worship him could do so. However, they had to appreciate that God was dealing with a congregated people and that His worship centered at a temple in Jerusalem. (1 Kings 8:41-43; Numbers 9:14) Persons could not be acceptable to God if they let pride or independence move them to devise their own way of worship.

A CHANGE IN CONGREGATIONS

[10] When Jesus engaged in his ministry on earth, God was still dealing with Israel as a people dedicated to him. Thus it was not necessary for everyone who accepted the Messiah to meet regularly with Jesus and travel with him as the apostles did. (Mark 5:18-20; 9:38-40) But the nation as a whole rejected Jehovah's Messiah, moving Jesus to say shortly before he died: "The kingdom of God will be taken from you and given

---

What change did God make in his dealings? (10-12)

to a people who will produce its fruit."—Matthew 21:43, *Jerusalem Bible*.

11 Who would this new people be, once the way of worship set out in God's law to Israel was no longer required? (Colossians 2:13, 14; Galatians 3:24, 25) On the day of Pentecost 33 C.E., the Christian congregation was formed and God made it clear to sincere observers that this was his doing. (Acts 2:1-4, 43-47; Hebrews 2:2-4) First, Jews and foreigners who had accepted Judaism, and, later, Gentiles, or people of the nations, became "a people for his name." God now considered them to be "a chosen race, a royal priesthood, a holy nation, a people for special possession."—Acts 15:14-18; 1 Peter 2:9, 10.

12 If you had lived then and wanted a relationship with God, you would have been directed to the Christian congregation. This is what happened with the Italian man Cornelius and his family. (Acts 10:1-48) The believers world wide constituted the Christian congregation. (1 Peter 5:9) All the local congregations, which met in homes or public buildings, were part of this one congregation that God was now using.—Acts 15:41; Romans 16:5.

13 Being a God of order, Jehovah arranged a measure of organization in the congregations. To provide needed attention to individual worshipers, he appointed men to serve as shepherds or overseers. They were experienced, qualified men who could teach God's Word and train members of the congregation to share Bible truth with others, to help in the vital work of preaching the "good news."—2 Timothy 2:1, 2; Ephesians 4:11-15; Matthew 24:14; Acts 20:28.

How did God organize and direct Christians? (13-15)

¹⁴ In many other ways, too, the congregations would benefit from these overseers. They were not to deal in a legalistic or oppressive manner. Rather, their assignment was lovingly to help fellow Christians to strengthen their relationship with God. (Acts 14:21-23; 1 Peter 5:2, 3) Any who had problems could go to these spiritually older men for kind, Scriptural help. (James 5:13-16; Isaiah 32:1, 2) Because Christians were still imperfect, occasionally difficulties might arise in congregations. The overseers were to be alert to help fellow Christians, and to be on guard against any who might endanger the congregation's spirituality.—Philippians 4:2, 3; 2 Timothy 4:2-5.

¹⁵ The congregations got needed directions from a Christian governing body of the apostles and older men of the Jerusalem congregation. They studied and resolved questions sent from congregations. And the governing body dispatched representatives to visit congregations.—Acts 15:1-3.

¹⁶ Jehovah God is still dealing with his people as a congregated group. Throughout the earth there are thousands of congregations of Jehovah's Witnesses. If you want to come into unity with God's way of worship, respond to his encouragement to congregate with fellow Christians:

> "Let us consider one another to incite to love and fine works, not forsaking the gathering of ourselves together, . . . but encouraging one another, and all the more so as you behold the day drawing near." —Hebrews 10:24, 25.

WORSHIPING GOD WHOLE-SOULED

¹⁷ It is good to reflect on all that Jehovah God

What meaning should God's way of dealing with Christians have for you? (16)

Love for God should move us to do what? (17-19)

has done for you. From him you have life and the provisions to sustain your life each day. On top of that, God sent his Son to earth to die as a sacrifice. That was an expression of God's deep love, love that is sure and constant. (Romans 5:8; 8:32, 38, 39) In that way God made it possible for you to gain forgiveness of sin and the prospect of everlasting life in happiness.—John 3:17; 17:3.

¹⁸ How will we respond to his love? Certainly we should not turn our back on God and his love. The apostle Peter urged:

"Repent, therefore, and turn around so as to get your sins blotted out, that seasons of refreshing may come."—Acts 3:19.

¹⁹ All of us need to "repent," for we have all sinned, fallen short of God's standards in our conduct, speech and thoughts. (Romans 2:4; 7: 14-21; James 3:2) For us to repent means to

recognize that we are sinners and to feel sorrow over our having failed to live in full harmony with Jehovah's will. Is that how you feel? Next, we need to "turn around," to change our way of life, henceforth striving to reflect Jehovah's qualities and to do things in his way. Doing that, we can trust that God will forgive and accept us.—Psalm 103:8-14; 2 Peter 3:9.

[20] Recognizing that Jesus provided a model so that we could follow his steps in serving God, we should endeavor to imitate his example. (1 Peter 2:21) Hebrews 10:7 tells us that Jesus' attitude was: "Look! I am come . . . to do your will, O God." Similarly, our love and appreciation for God should move us to dedicate our lives to him, to do his will whole-souled. Of course, we will still eat, sleep, care for and love our family, enjoy pleasant relaxation and in other ways share in the normal activities of life. But dedicating our lives to God means that his will and worship should be of primary importance, and that, no matter where we are or what we are doing, we will earnestly endeavor to apply God's counsel and follow the example Jesus set.—Colossians 3:23, 24.

[21] The Scriptures make clear that a person who dedicates his life to God should publicly manifest that by being baptized. Jesus told his followers:

> "Go therefore and make disciples of people of all the nations, *baptizing* them in the name of the Father and of the Son and of the holy spirit, *teaching them to observe* all the things I have commanded you."—Matthew 28:19, 20.

If those getting baptized were to have studied God's Word and become disciples of Christ, then

---

Why is baptism an important step, and what does it symbolize? (20, 21)

clearly they were not mere infants. Also, their baptism, in symbol of their dedication to God, was by total immersion in water, as Jesus was baptized in the Jordan River.—Mark 1:9-11; Acts 8:36-39.

²² Your becoming a baptized disciple of Christ will put you in line for the full and happy life of real Christianity. It is not a life governed by endless do's and don'ts. Rather, it is a life of satisfying growth. You can steadily improve your spiritual outlook and your application of God's Word, this bringing you ever closer to the example Jesus set.—Philippians 1:9-11; Ephesians 1:15-19.

²³ This will affect your daily thinking and conduct. As you pursue the Christian way, your conviction will deepen that soon God will destroy all wickedness, making way for 'a new heavens and a new earth in which righteousness is to dwell.' This, in turn, will increase your motivation to develop the Christian personality and to pursue the way of life that will enable you to find a place in that coming new order. (Ephesians 4:17, 22-24) The apostle Peter was inspired to write:

> "Think what sort of people you ought to be, what devout and dedicated lives you should live! With this [new order] to look forward to, do your utmost to be found at peace with him, unblemished and above reproach in his sight."—2 Peter 3:11, 14, *New English Bible*.

²⁴ What a blessing when a person's entire life reflects the fact that he is worshiping Jehovah God! Though today many are living just to please themselves and selfishly to get all the pleasures they can, you can live and worship the true God in his way. This is the best way of life.

Have you dedicated your life to God, and do you want to be baptized? What will this mean for you? (22-24)

20

What Kind of Life Do You Want?

IF SOMEONE asked you, 'How can I find happiness today?' what would be your answer? You might say with conviction: 'For a full, happy and enduring life, do things God's way!'

² In previous chapters we have considered that the Creator truly does exist, that he offers through the Bible information and guidance that we all need, and that applying his Word is practical today. Living as true Christians can help us to cope with problems such as stress and loneliness. Looking to the Bible for guidance can safeguard us against painful problems caused by drunkenness, immorality, dishonesty and other vices. (Proverbs 4:11-13) Adopting the Bible's outlook on money enables us to be more content and to "get a firm hold on the real life."—1 Timothy 6:19.

³ When we take heed to what the Creator says, our life gains meaning and direction. We understand why God has permitted wickedness and suffering. And as we discern the fulfillment of Bible prophecies in the events of our day, we realize that we are living in the "last days" of the present wicked system of things. (2 Timothy 3:1-5) That means that *soon* God will eliminate all human kingdoms with their history of political

---

POINT FOR DISCUSSION: Why is doing things God's way the best means of finding happiness? (1-3)

corruption and armed forces maintained by crushing tax burdens. (Daniel 2:44; Revelation 16:14, 16) Thus God will end the succession of human efforts to rule the earth and will direct surviving mankind by means of his heavenly kingdom.—Revelation 11:17, 18; 21:1-4.

IS THAT WHAT YOU WANT?

⁴ Most of us would say: 'It would be wonderful to live among loving, God-fearing persons in paradise.' (Isaiah 11:9) But to do so our love of righteousness and our desire to conform to God's standards must be strong enough to determine the overall pattern of our life now. (Matthew 12:34; 15:19) Is that what you truly *want?* In this regard, the disciple James was inspired to write Christians:

"Do you not know that the friendship with the world is enmity with God? Whoever, therefore, WANTS to be a friend of the world is constituting himself an enemy of God."—James 4:4.

⁵ James also stressed that "the form of worship that is clean and undefiled from the standpoint of our God" involves 'keeping oneself without spot from the world.' (James 1:27) We should strive to do that. Of course, since Christians are living among the world's violence and corruption, its immoral schemes, politics and nationalism, it is not easy to remain 100 percent unaffected. Even the most devoted Christian may slip or make mistakes while trying to avoid being stained by the world's way. That is why Christians need to continue working to improve. (Colossians 3:5-10) But the point is, what do we *want?*

Why must we decide whether we want to be a friend of the world or of God? (4-6)

[6] As an illustration, we might imagine two men who are eating dinner. One man accidentally gets a spot of gravy on his tie. The other takes his tie and deliberately dips it into the gravy; he wants it that way. Which one are we like? By what we allow to influence us and what we choose to do, are we showing that we *want* to be a friend of the world? or a friend of God?

[7] Friendship with the world can be reflected in many ways. Some persons are so strongly attached to their family or neighbors that they go along with, even sharing in, things they know God disapproves of, such as unscriptural celebrations, heavy drinking, obscene jesting or showing racial prejudice. (1 Peter 4:3, 4; Ephesians 5:3-5; Acts 10:34, 35) If we *want* to please God, then having his approval will mean more to us than even that of our relatives.—Luke 14:26, 27; 11:23.

[8] Similarly, our choice of entertainment may give indication of whether we want to be a friend of the world. The early Christians would not attend brutal gladiatorial fights or watch plays highlighting immorality. What about us today? We ought to think about our preferences as to sports, television programs, motion pictures or reading matter. If we discern that we are being conditioned to *want* what God counsels against, we need to work at reshaping our preferences. The allurement of the world can affect even young persons who have grown up in Christian families and Christians who have long studied the Bible.

[9] This matter of friendship with God or friend-

In what ways might a person manifest whether he wants friendship with the world? (7, 8)

How important is it for us to determine what we really want? (9-12)

ship with the world means life or death. (1 John 2:15-17) We can no more keep a foot on both sides than a person at a fork in the road can walk down two diverging paths.

¹⁰ During the days of Elijah, some Hebrews were affected by the Baal worship of surrounding nations. Even though having some connection with the true God, Jehovah, they did not hold to him completely. Elijah said that they were "limping upon two different opinions." They had to decide whether they would adhere to Jehovah and his ways or not. It was a choice meaning life or death.—1 Kings 18:21-40; Deuteronomy 30:19, 20.

¹¹ We cannot postpone deciding what we really want. In the first century C.E., the apostle Peter urged Christians to 'keep close in mind the presence of the day of Jehovah' in which wickedness on earth will be destroyed. Their sense of urgency was to be reflected by "holy acts of conduct and deeds of godly devotion," including the enthusiastic declaring of the Christian message. (2 Peter 3:11, 12) While some Christians lived exemplary married lives, others chose to remain unmarried so that they could give 'constant attention to the Lord without distraction.'—1 Corinthians 7:29-35.

¹² If the kind of life Christians wanted to live was important in the first century, how much more vital a matter it is now! We can see that God's kingdom is already ruling in heaven and that there is but "a short period of time" left before God through Christ will crush the nations and bind Satan the Devil. (Revelation 12:12; 19:11–20:2) So now is the time to decide what kind of life we want.

THE KIND OF LIFE GOD WILL PROVIDE

[13] The kind of life we choose now will determine whether we will be allowed to enjoy the kind of life God will provide in the coming new order.

[14] It is easy to think first of the many physical blessings of the restored paradise. In the original paradise, Adam and Eve had ample nutritious food. (Genesis 2:9, 16) Thus, in the new order there will be good, healthful food in abundance. —Psalm 72:16; 67:6.

[15] Adam and Eve had good health, for God created them perfect. That underscores the Bible's assurance that in the new order sickness, disease-caused pain and tears of sorrow will be things of the past. (Revelation 21:1-4) Mankind will grow to physical perfection.

[16] No longer hindered by problems and then death after 70 years, men and women will have the thrill of being able to investigate many fields of learning and experience. You will be able to enjoy the full expression of your talents, even developing some that you never guessed you had. Cooking, home building, cabinet-making, decorating, gardening, playing musical instruments, tailoring, studying the vast fields of knowledge— You could go on and on listing the challenging and beneficial things you will be able to do. Jehovah once said: "The work of their own hands my chosen ones will use to the full."—Isaiah 65:22.

[17] Also, the Bible says that in the garden of Eden the diet of the animals was vegetation. (Genesis 1:30) Hence, you can look forward to God's arranging matters so that the animals will no longer be ferocious and dangerous; they will be

What kind of life will God provide in the new order? (13-18)

Time to develop and use your talents to the full

at peace with one another and with humans. Both children and grown-ups will enjoy their companionship to the full.—Compare Isaiah 11:6-8; 65:25; Hosea 2:18.

[18] But the Bible does not begin to describe in detail all the material blessings of the new order. Jehovah, our Creator, knows our needs. The Bible assures us about God: "You are opening your hand and satisfying the desire of every living thing."—Psalm 145:16.

[19] The Scriptures properly emphasize, not the material prosperity or blessings, but the spiritual and mental things that will make for happiness

What are the more important blessings promised for the restored paradise? (19, 20)

in the restored paradise. For example, we can look forward to conditions as described this way:

> "The work of the true righteousness must become peace; and the service of the true righteousness, quietness and security to time indefinite. And my people must dwell in a peaceful abiding place and in residences of full confidence and in undisturbed resting-places."—Isaiah 32:17, 18.

[20] We can appreciate that even if we had good health, a fine home and abundant food, we would not be truly contented if we were surrounded by conflict, tension, jealousy and wrath. (Proverbs 15:17; 21:9) However, the persons God permits to live in the coming paradise will be those who have conscientiously worked at overcoming such human failings. They will form a worldwide family of Christians who cultivate the fruits of God's spirit, including love, peace, kindness and self-control. (Galatians 5:19-23) They will sincerely strive to have personalities that harmonize with Jehovah's personality.—Ephesians 4:22-24.

LIVING TO PLEASE AND PRAISE JEHOVAH

[21] The foretold material and spiritual blessings give us reason to look forward to the new order. However, if we let those be the *primary* reasons for worshiping God and living a Christian life, to some extent we would be like the present me-first generation who are concerned foremost about what *they* want and can get.

[22] Rather, we should cultivate a desire to live a Christian life—now and in the future—because *God* wants us to do so. He should come first, not we. Jesus showed the view we need, saying: "I am come . . . to do your will, O God," and, "My

How may we find real happiness? (21-24)

food is for me to do the will of him that sent me and to finish his work." (Hebrews 10:7; John 4:34) Appreciation for what God has done should move us to put him first.—Romans 5:8.

²³ Appropriately, the Bible does not stress as of foremost importance our salvation and the blessings we can receive. Rather, it emphasizes the vindication of God's name and the rightness of our praising God for what he is and what he has done. David wrote:

"I will exalt you, O my God the King, and I will bless your name to time indefinite, even forever. Jehovah is great and very much to be praised, and his greatness is unsearchable. The glorious splendor of your dignity and the matters of your wonderful works I will make my concern."—Psalm 145:1, 3, 5.

²⁴ Putting God first in life and actively praising him was fitting for Jesus and for David. It is also very fitting for us. When we combine this with the practical Christian way of life, we will have found happiness—now and into the lasting future.

You have now considered many of the Bible's basic and important teachings. We would encourage you to continue to grow in knowledge of God's Word. Aids in your doing this are:

The Bible—God's Word or Man's?

Making Your Family Life Happy

Questions Young People Ask—Answers That Work

These Bible study aids can be obtained from Jehovah's Witnesses in your area. Or you can receive them by writing Watch Tower, using the appropriate address on the next page.

Would you welcome more information or a free home Bible study?

Write Watch Tower at appropriate address below.

ALASKA 99507: 2552 East 48th Ave., Anchorage. **ALBANIA:** Kutia Postare 3, Tiranë. **ARGENTINA:** Elcano 3820, 1427 Buenos Aires. **AUSTRALIA:** Box 280, Ingleburn, N.S.W. 2565. **AUSTRIA:** Postfach 67, A-1134 Vienna [13 Gallgasse 42-44, Vienna]. **BAHAMAS:** Box N-1247, Nassau, N.P. **BARBADOS:** Fontabelle Rd., Bridgetown. **BELGIUM:** rue d'Argile-Potaardestraat 60, B-1950 Kraainem. **BELIZE:** Box 257, Belize City. **BENIN, REP. OF:** Box 06-1131, Cotonou. **BOLIVIA:** Casilla No. 1440, La Paz. **BRAZIL:** Caixa Postal 92, 18270-970 Tatuí, SP. **BULGARIA:** P.K. 353, Sofia 1000. **CANADA:** Box 4100, Halton Hills (Georgetown), Ontario L7G 4Y4. **CENTRAL AFRICAN REPUBLIC:** B.P. 662, Bangui. **CHILE:** Casilla 267, Puente Alto [Av. Concha y Toro 3456, Puente Alto]. **COLOMBIA:** Apartado Aéreo 85058, Bogotá 8, D.E. **COSTA RICA:** Apartado 10043, San José. **CÔTE D'IVOIRE (IVORY COAST), WEST AFRICA:** 06 B P 393, Abidjan 06. **CROATIA:** p.p. 417, 41001 Zagreb. **CYPRUS:** P. O. Box 33, Dhali, Nicosia. **CZECHIA:** pošt. př. 65, 140 00 Praha 4. **DENMARK:** Stenhusvej 28, DK-4300 Holbæk. **DOMINICAN REPUBLIC:** Apartado 1742, Santo Domingo. **ECUADOR:** Casilla 09-01-4512, Guayaquil. **EL SALVADOR:** Apartado Postal 401, San Salvador. **ENGLAND:** The Ridgeway, London NW7 1RP. **FIJI:** Box 23, Suva. **FINLAND:** Postbox 68, SF-01301 Vantaa 30. **FRANCE:** B.P. 63, F-92105 Boulogne-Billancourt Cedex. **FRENCH GUIANA:** 15 rue Chawari, Cogneau Larivot, 97351 Matoury. **GERMANY:** Niederselters, Am Steinfels, D-65618 Selters. **GHANA:** Box 760, Accra. **GREECE:** P.O. Box 112, GR-322 00 Thiva. **GUADELOUPE:** Monmain, 97180 Sainte Anne. **GUAM 96913:** 143 Jehovah St., Barrigada. **GUATEMALA:** 17 Calle 13-63, Zona 11, 01011 Guatemala. **GUYANA:** 50 Brickdam, Georgetown 16. **HAITI:** Post Box 185, Port-au-Prince. **HAWAII 96819:** 2055 Kam IV Rd., Honolulu. **HONDURAS:** Apartado 147, Tegucigalpa. **HONG KONG:** 4 Kent Road, Kowloon Tong. **HUNGARY:** Pf. 223, H-1425 Budapest. **ICELAND:** P. O. Box 8496, IS-128 Reykjavík. **INDIA:** Post Bag 10, Lonavla, Pune Dis., Mah. 410 401. **IRELAND:** 29A Jamestown Road, Finglas, Dublin 11. **ISRAEL:** P. O. Box 961, 61-009 Tel Aviv. **ITALY:** Via della Bufalotta 1281, I-00138 Rome RM. **JAMAICA:** Box 180, Kingston 10. **JAPAN:** 1271 Nakashinden, Ebina City, Kanagawa Pref., 243-04. **KENYA:** Box 47788, Nairobi. **KOREA, REPUBLIC OF:** Box 33 Pyungtaek P. O., Kyunggido, 450-600. **LEEWARD ISLANDS:** Box 119, St. Johns, Antigua. **LIBERIA:** P.O. Box 10-0380, 1000 Monrovia 10. **LUXEMBOURG:** B. P. 2186, L-1021 Luxembourg, G. D. **MADAGASCAR:** B.P. 511, Antananarivo 101. **MALAYSIA:** 28 Jalan Kampar, Off Jalan Landasan, 41300 Klang, Sel. **MARTINIQUE:** Cours Campeche, Morne Tartenson, 97200 Fort de France. **MAURITIUS:** Box 54, Vacoas. **MEXICO:** Apartado Postal 896, 06002 Mexico, D. F. **MOZAMBIQUE:** Caixa Postal 2600, Maputo. **MYANMAR:** P.O. Box 62, Yangon. **NETHERLANDS:** Noordbargerstraat 77, NL-7812 AA Emmen. **NETHERLANDS ANTILLES:** P.O. Box 4708, Willemstad, Curaçao. **NEW CALEDONIA:** B.P. 787, Nouméa. **NEW ZEALAND:** P.O. Box 142, Manurewa. **NICARAGUA:** Apartado 3587, Managua. **NIGERIA:** P.M.B. 1090, Benin City, Edo State. **NORWAY:** Gaupeveien 24, N-1914 Ytre Enebakk. **PAKISTAN:** 197-A Ahmad Block, New Garden Town, Lahore 54600. **PANAMA:** Apartado 6-2671, Zona 6A, El Dorado. **PAPUA NEW GUINEA:** Box 636, Boroko, N.C.D. **PARAGUAY:** Díaz de Solís 1485 esq. C.A. López, Sajonia, Asunción. **PERU:** Casilla 18-1055, Lima [Av. El Cortijo 329, Monterrico Chico, Lima 33]. **PHILIPPINES, REPUBLIC OF:** P. O. Box 2044, 1099 Manila [186 Roosevelt Ave., San Francisco del Monte, 1105 Quezon City]. **POLAND:** Skr. Poczt. 13, PL-05-830 Nadarzyn. **PORTUGAL:** Apartado 91, P-2766 Estoril Codex [Rua Cooba Barão, 511, Alcabideche, P-2765 Estoril]. **PUERTO RICO 00970:** P.O. Box 3980, Guaynabo. **ROMANIA:** Str. Parfumului 22, RO-74121, Bucharest. **RUSSIA:** ul. Tankistov, 4, Solnechnoye, Sestroretzky Rayon, 189640 St. Petersburg. **SENEGAL:** B.P. 3107, Dakar. **SIERRA LEONE, WEST AFRICA:** P. O. Box 136, Freetown. **SLOVAKIA:** P.O. Box 17, 810 00 Bratislava 1. **SOLOMON ISLANDS:** P.O. Box 166, Honiara. **SOUTH AFRICA:** Private Bag X2067, Krugersdorp, 1740. **SPAIN:** Apartado postal 132, E-28850 Torrejón de Ardoz (Madrid). **SRI LANKA, REP. OF:** 62 Layard's Road, Colombo 5. **SURINAME:** P. O. Box 49, Paramaribo. **SWEDEN:** Box 5, S-732 21 Arboga. **SWITZERLAND:** P.O. Box 225, CH-3602 Thun [Ulmenweg 45, Thun]. **TAHITI:** B.P. 518, Papeete. **TAIWAN:** 107 Yun Ho Street, Taipei 10613. **THAILAND:** 69/1 Soi Phasuk, Sukhumwit Rd., Soi 2, Bangkok 10110. **TOGO:** B.P. 4460, Lome. **TRINIDAD AND TOBAGO, REP. OF:** Lower Rapsey Street & Laxmi Lane, Curepe. **UKRAINE:** P.O. Box 246, 290000 Lviv. **UNITED STATES OF AMERICA:** 25 Columbia Heights, Brooklyn, N.Y. 11201. **URUGUAY:** Francisco Bauzá 3372, 11600 Montevideo. **VENEZUELA:** Apartado 20.364, Caracas, DF 1020A [Av. La Victoria; cruce con 17 de diciembre, La Victoria, Edo. Aragua 2121A]. **WESTERN SAMOA:** P. O. Box 673, Apia. **YUGOSLAVIA, F.R.:** Milorada Mitrovića 4, YU-11 000 Belgrade. **ZAIRE, REP. OF:** B.P. 634, Limete, Kinshasa. **ZAMBIA:** Box 33459, Lusaka 10101. **ZIMBABWE:** 35 Fife Avenue, Harare.